Simply Social at School

Written by Angie Neal, M.S., CCC-SLP and Rynette R. Kjesbo, M.S., CCC-SLP
Illustrated by Mark Bristol

Copyright © 2011 by SUPER DUPER® PUBLICATIONS,
a division of Super Duper®, Inc. All rights reserved.

Permission is granted for the user to reproduce the material contained herein in limited form for classroom use only. Reproduction of this material for an entire school or school system is strictly prohibited. No part of this material may be reproduced (except as noted above), stored in a retrieval system, or transmitted in any form or by any means (mechanically, electronically, recording, web, etc.) without the prior written consent and approval of Super Duper® Publications.

Printed in the United States

ISBN 978-1-60723-005-2

Super Duper® Publications
www.superduperinc.com
Post Office Box 24997 • Greenville, SC 29616 USA
1-800-277-8737 • Fax 1-800-978-7379

How to Use *Simply Social 7™ at School*

Simply Social 7™ at School teaches fifty social skills that may be challenging for students with pragmatic difficulties. Topics range from everyday skills such as *following directions, using greetings,* and *turn-taking* to more complex skills like *giving advice, understanding figurative language,* and *understanding facial expressions.* Within each topic students learn about the skill and then apply the skill by completing extension activities.

Each topic has a *Simply Social 7 Steps* page which is a set of seven practical steps for students to think about while working on the skill. As the teacher reads each step in the *Simply Social 7*, students respond by reading or repeating the statements in italics that follow.

A *Look and Learn* page follows each lesson. A humorous cartoon scene illustrates the social skill for that section. Each scene shows students who are using the social skill appropriately and students who are not. Students can use this page to identify the skill they are working on and to discuss what the students in the scene are doing correctly and what they could improve.

Students apply what they learned using the *Think and Review* page. This page presents different social situations in the classroom, at school, at home, and in the community. Students use their knowledge and reasoning skills to determine if the students in the situations are making good choices or poor choices. Students can then discuss what the students in the situations should do next or what they could do differently.

Finally send the *Take-Home Practice* page home with the students to let parents know what skill(s) their children are working on. The *Take-Home Practice* page gives parents a practical way to review the social skill(s) with their children and gives students an opportunity to reinforce what they learned. Teachers and therapists can customize the *Parent/Helper Letter* (p. vi) to explain to parents how to help their children practice these skills.

Awards and Motivation

As students learn each social skill, they can add their signed practice pages to a folder or notebook to create their own *Simply Social Skills Book*. Students can review their individual *Simply Social Skills Book* at any time to refresh social skills that they learned. There is a *Simply Social Superstar* award at the bottom of the *Take-Home Practice* page for each topic. Students become a *Simply Social Superstar* when they demonstrate mastery of a social skill. When a student earns a *Simply Social Superstar* award, attach it to a blank page in the student's individual *Simply Social Skills Book* or display it on a wall in his/her classroom, therapy room, or home.

Social Skills Checklist

Simply Social 7™ at School includes a checklist for use in identifying a student's social strengths and weaknesses. Up to three people (SLP/Educator, another professional, and a parent/caregiver) may complete the checklist as a pretest to measure a student's baseline performance and identify areas of weakness to target for remediation. After using the *Simply Social 7 Steps* to teach the fifty skills and giving students the opportunity to apply their knowledge with the activities on the *Look and Learn*, *Think and Review*, and *Take-Home Practice* pages, use the checklist again as a posttest to measure the overall effectiveness of the social-skills interventions.

Simply Social 7 — Table of Contents

Introduction iii

Parent/Helper Letter vi

Social Skills Checklist Summary (SLP/Educator Form) .... vii–x

Social Skills Checklist (Observer Form) .... xi–xiv

Introductory Skills 1–28

Being Aware of Your Surroundings 1–4

Making Eye Contact 5–8

Using Manners 9–12

Being a Good Listener 13–16

Using an Appropriate Rate of Speech 17–20

Using an Appropriate Volume 21–24

Respecting Personal Space 25–28

Conversational Skills 29–80

Using Greetings 29–32

Starting a Conversation 33–36

Joining a Conversation 37–40

Expressing Opinions 41–44

Giving Enough Information 45–48

Asking for More Information 49–52

Staying on Topic 53–56

Switching Topics 57–60

Interrupting 61–64

Using Gestures 65–68

Interpreting Body Language 69–72

Ending a Conversation 73–76

Adjusting Your Language Level 77–80

Academic Skills 81–120

Following Rules 81–84

Paying Attention 85–88

Ignoring Distractions 89–92

Getting the Teacher's Attention 93–96

Asking for Permission 97–100

Asking Questions 101–104

Answering Questions 105–108

Following Directions 109–112

Dealing with Transition 113–116

Understanding Figurative Language 117–120

Simply Social 7 — Table of Contents

Relationship Skills 121–152
Making Friends 121–124
Maintaining Friendships 125–128
Taking Another's Perspective 129–132
Giving Advice 133–136
Turn-Taking 137–140
Asking for Help 141–144
Helping Others 145–148
Working with Others in a Group 149–152

Conflict Management Skills 153–176
Accepting "No" 153–156
Accepting Consequences 157–160
Accepting Discipline 161–164
Accepting Constructive Criticism 165–168
Dealing with Failure 169–172
Resolving Conflict 173–176

Emotional Communication Skills 177–200
Understanding Facial Expressions 177–180
Understanding Emotions 181–184
Expressing Feelings 185–188
Dealing with Anger 189–192
Using Humor 193–196
Dealing with Change 197–200

#BK-371 Simply Social 7™ at School • ©2011 Super Duper® Publications • www.superduperinc.com • 1-800-277-8737

Simply Social 7™ — Parent/Helper Letter

Dear Parent/Helper,

_____ is currently learning about social skills. Social skills are the behaviors we use
(Child's Name)

when we communicate and interact with other people. Social skills help us to get along and work well
with others.

Today your child learned about _____. We talked about
(Social Skill)

seven simple steps to think about when using this social skill. We call these the **Simply Social 7.**

The attached worksheet will help your child practice and reinforce the **Simply Social 7.** Your child will
bring home more of these worksheets throughout the year.

☐   After you review the **Simply Social 7** with your child, please sign and return the page by
    _____. We will create a *Simply Social Skills Book* for your child to keep his/her
    (Date)
    completed pages in and will add this page to his/her book.

☐   Please review the **Simply Social 7** with your child. You do not need to return the page. Please
    create your own *Simply Social Skills Book* at home by adding each new skill page to a folder
    or notebook.

☐   _____

    _____

    _____

Thank you for your support!

_____   _____
Teacher/SLP Signature   Date

_____   _____
Parent/Helper Signature   Date

Simply Social 7™ Social Skills Checklist Summary   1

(SLP/Educator Form)

Student's Name:	Age/Grade:
Examiner's Name:	Date Form Completed:

This checklist can help you decide which lessons to use with your student(s).

1. Give a copy of the *Social Skills Checklist* on pp. xi–xiv to two observers — preferably one of the student's teachers and a parent/caregiver.

2. After the two observers return the completed checklists, observe the child and complete a third checklist.

3. Use this *Social Skills Checklist Summary* (pp. vii-x) to total all of the "Yes" and "No" responses for each social skill.

4. Total scores with two or more "No" responses are areas of concern.

Introductory Skills							
Social Skill	**Observer 1**		**Observer 2**		**Observer 3**		**Total "No"**
	Yes	**No**	**Yes**	**No**	**Yes**	**No**	
Being Aware of Your Surroundings (p. 1)							
Making Eye Contact (p. 5)							
Using Manners (p. 9)							
Being a Good Listener (p. 13)							
Using an Appropriate Rate of Speech (p. 17)							
Using an Appropriate Volume (p. 21)							
Respecting Personal Space (p. 25)							

<u>**Introductory Skills Comments:**</u>

#BK-371 Simply Social 7™ at School • ©2011 Super Duper® Publications • www.superduperinc.com • 1-800-277-8737   vii

Simply Social 7™ Social Skills Checklist Summary 2

Conversational Skills							
Social Skill	**Observer 1**		**Observer 2**		**Observer 3**		**Total "No"**
	Yes	No	Yes	No	Yes	No	
Using Greetings (p. 29)							
Starting a Conversation (p. 33)							
Joining a Conversation (p. 37)							
Expressing Opinions (p. 41)							
Giving Enough Information (p. 45)							
Asking for More Information (p. 49)							
Staying on Topic (p. 53)							
Switching Topics (p. 57)							
Interrupting (p. 61)							
Using Gestures (p. 65)							
Interpreting Body Language (p. 69)							
Ending a Conversation (p. 73)							
Adjusting Your Language Level (p. 77)							

Conversational Skills Comments:

viii   #BK-371 Simply Social 7™ at School • ©2011 Super Duper® Publications • www.superduperinc.com • 1-800-277-8737

Simply Social 7™ — Social Skills Checklist Summary ③

Academic Skills							
Social Skill	**Observer 1**		**Observer 2**		**Observer 3**		
	Yes	**No**	**Yes**	**No**	**Yes**	**No**	**Total "No"**
Following Rules (p. 81)							
Paying Attention (p. 85)							
Ignoring Distractions (p. 89)							
Getting the Teacher's Attention (p. 93)							
Asking for Permission (p. 97)							
Asking Questions (p. 101)							
Answering Questions (p. 105)							
Following Directions (p. 109)							
Dealing with Transition (p. 113)							
Understanding Figurative Language (p. 117)							

Academic Skills Comments:

Relationship Skills							
Social Skill	**Observer 1**		**Observer 2**		**Observer 3**		
	Yes	**No**	**Yes**	**No**	**Yes**	**No**	**Total "No"**
Making Friends (p. 121)							
Maintaining Friendships (p. 125)							
Taking Another's Perspective (p. 129)							
Giving Advice (p. 133)							
Turn-Taking (p. 137)							
Asking for Help (p. 141)							
Helping Others (p. 145)							
Working with Others in a Group (p. 149)							

Relationship Skills Comments:

#BK-371 Simply Social 7™ at School • ©2011 Super Duper® Publications • www.superduperinc.com • 1-800-277-8737

Simply Social 7™ — Social Skills Checklist Summary — 4

Conflict Management Skills

Social Skill	Observer 1		Observer 2		Observer 3		
	Yes	No	Yes	No	Yes	No	Total "No"
Accepting "No" (p. 153)							
Accepting Consequences (p. 157)							
Accepting Discipline (p. 161)							
Accepting Constructive Criticism (p. 165)							
Dealing with Failure (p. 169)							
Resolving Conflict (p. 173)							

Conflict Management Skills Comments:

Emotional Communication Skills

Social Skill	Observer 1		Observer 2		Observer 3		
	Yes	No	Yes	No	Yes	No	Total "No"
Understanding Facial Expressions (p. 177)							
Understanding Emotions (p. 181)							
Expressing Feelings (p. 185)							
Dealing with Anger (p. 189)							
Using Humor (p. 193)							
Dealing with Change (p. 197)							

Emotional Communication Skills Comments:

#BK-371 Simply Social 7™ at School • ©2011 Super Duper® Publications • www.superduperinc.com • 1-800-277-8737

Social Skills Checklist

(Observer Form)

Student's Name: _____ Age/Grade: _____

Observer's Name: _____ Date Form Completed: _____
❏ SLP   ❏ Parent   ❏ Teacher   ❏ Other

Directions: Please read each statement and check "yes" if it applies to the student, or "no" if it does not apply.

	Introductory Skills		
Social Skill Page #	**Behavior**	**Yes**	**No**
1	Stays safe by being mindful of what is going on around him/her		
5	Looks at others without staring during conversation		
9	Uses polite words such as "please," "thank you," and "excuse me"		
13	Listens and pays attention while others are talking		
17	Speaks at a rate of speech that the listener(s) can understand, not speaking too fast nor too slow		
21	Speaks at a normal volume without speaking too loudly or too softly		
25	Stands or sits near others without getting too close		

Introductory Skills Comments:

#BK-371 Simply Social 7™ at School • ©2011 Super Duper® Publications • www.superduperinc.com • 1-800-277-8737   xi

Conversational Skills

Social Skill Page #	Behavior	Yes	No
29	Says "hello" when meeting someone and "goodbye" when parting		
33	Greets others and makes small talk to begin conversations		
37	Joins conversations without dominating the discussion, being aggressive, or going off topic		
41	Shares feelings and beliefs about something and shows respect for others' opinions		
45	Gives enough information about the topic so that the listener(s) can follow the conversation		
49	Recognizes when a speaker's message is not understood and asks for more information to clarify		
53	Participates in conversations without going off topic		
57	Uses smooth transitions to change subjects during conversation		
61	Interrupts only when necessary and uses polite manners when interrupting		
65	Uses appropriate gestures to add information to his/her message		
69	Understands the meaning of others' gestures, posture, and facial expressions		
73	Knows when to end a conversation and ends the talk in a positive way		
77	Changes the way something is said so that the listener(s) understands		

Conversational Skills Comments:

Social Skills Checklist

	Academic Skills		
Social Skill Page #	**Behavior**	**Yes**	**No**
81	Knows the rules and follows them		
85	Pays attention to a speaker and refocuses when attention is lost		
89	Remains focused on tasks even when distractions are present		
93	Gets the teacher's attention without interrupting inappropriately, such as blurting out		
97	Asks permission to do things and accepts the decision		
101	Asks specific questions to get needed information		
105	Provides answers that are clear and relevant to the topic		
109	Listens to directions and follows through to complete a task		
113	Changes from one activity to another without difficulty		
117	Understands figures of speech (similes, metaphors, etc.) and does not take them literally		

Academic Skills Comments:

	Relationship Skills		
Social Skill Page #	**Behavior**	**Yes**	**No**
121	Develops friendships by being pleasant and friendly		
125	Accepts others for who they are and works through problems to maintain friendships		
129	Sees situations from someone else's point of view		
133	Gives helpful and appropriate advice when asked		
137	Requests turns politely and shares with others to give turns with desired objects or activities		
141	Recognizes the need for help and requests specific help before becoming frustrated		
145	Offers assistance when others need help and assists others when asked		
149	Works with others cooperatively, doing his/her share of the work		

Relationship Skills Comments:

Social Skills Checklist

Conflict Management Skills

Social Skill Page #	Behavior	Yes	No
153	Accepts "no" for an answer without getting frustrated the first time it is stated		
157	Accepts consequences for actions without getting angry or having a tantrum		
161	Accepts discipline for behavior or actions without getting angry or talking back		
165	Accepts positive (constructive) criticism and negative criticism without getting angry or upset		
169	Doesn't make excuses and tries to learn from mistakes		
173	Works with others to develop solutions to conflict(s)		

Conflict Management Skills Comments:

Emotional Communication Skills

Social Skill Page #	Behavior	Yes	No
177	Uses facial expressions that match the words being said		
181	Understands his/her own emotions and expresses them in ways that are helpful and not hurtful to others		
185	Expresses positive and negative feelings in ways that are helpful and not hurtful		
189	Remains calm and deals with anger in positive ways		
193	Uses humor at appropriate times and does not use humor to hurt others		
197	Remains positive and sees the "big picture" when faced with change		

Emotional Communication Skills Comments:

Simply Social 7: Being Aware of Your Surroundings

Simply Social 7 Steps

Teacher says: Being aware of your surroundings means knowing what's going on around you. It's a way of keeping you and others around you safe. When you know who and what is beside, in front of, and behind you, you are less likely to have an accident.

Directions: Teacher will read the **Simply Social 7** steps. Student(s) will read or repeat the statements in italics that follow.

1 **Remove objects that may distract you** – A *distraction* is anything that keeps you from focusing on a task. When you are distracted, you are not always aware of what is going on around you.

I will put distracting things away.

2 **Don't fool around** – Goofing around with friends can distract you and keep your attention away from your surroundings.

I will not goof around with my friends.

3 **Know your purpose** – When you know where you're going and what you're doing, you can pay more attention to what is going on around you.

I will think about where I am going and what I am doing.

4 **Know who is around you** – Being aware of the people around you and knowing where they are can keep you from bumping into someone.

I will be aware of the people around me.

5 **Look for potential danger** – Look around for anything that may be unsafe.

I will look for things that might be unsafe.

6 **Listen** – Listen to nearby sounds to determine what is happening around you.

I will listen to the people and noises around me.

7 **Use caution around corners** – Because you cannot see what is around the corner, it is a good idea to be careful when you approach one.

I will slow down when going around corners.

#BK-371 Simply Social 7™ at School • ©2011 Super Duper® Publications • www.superduperinc.com • 1-800-277-8737

Simply Social 7: Being Aware of Your Surroundings

Look and Learn

Teacher says: The students in this scene are leaving school at the end of the day.

Directions: 1. **Draw a circle** around each student who **is aware of his/her surroundings**.

2. **Draw an X** on each student who **is not aware of his/her surroundings**.

Simply Social 7 — Being Aware of Your Surroundings

Think and Review

Directions: Read the stories, and then answer the questions below about the **Simply Social 7** for **Being Aware of Your Surroundings**.

1. **In the classroom...** Eli was playing with the buttons on his watch when the teacher told the class to line up. Eli wanted to adjust the time on his watch, so he continued to play with the buttons as he walked toward the door.

    Did Eli do the right thing?
    a) Yes – What could he do next?
    b) No – What should he have done?

2. **At school...** Brian was late for class so he was hurrying through the hallway. As he approached the corner of the hallway, he didn't notice the sound of students coming from the other side.

    Did Brian do the right thing?
    a) Yes – What could he do next?
    b) No – What should he have done?

3. **At home...** Valerie opened the door to go outside and noticed some movement in the tall grass. She decided to stop walking to see what the movement was. As Valerie waited, a rattlesnake moved across the sidewalk where she was about to walk.

    Did Valerie do the right thing?
    a) Yes – What could she do next?
    b) No – What should she have done?

4. **In the community...** Lillian was leaving the doctor's office with her mom. As they walked through the parking lot toward the car, Lillian started digging through her purse looking for a piece of gum.

    Did Lillian do the right thing?
    a) Yes – What could she do next?
    b) No – What should she have done?

Discussion Questions

1. What are some situations in which you had to be aware of your surroundings?

2. What would happen if you didn't pay attention to what was going on around you while crossing the street?

#BK-371 Simply Social 7™ at School • ©2011 Super Duper® Publications • www.superduperinc.com • 1-800-277-8737

Simply Social 7: Being Aware of Your Surroundings

Take-Home Practice

Dear Parent/Helper,

Today we talked about seven steps to follow while being aware of your surroundings called the **Simply Social 7**. Please review these with your child. Have him/her read or repeat the statement in italics that follows each step. Then sign, date, and return this page. We will add this page to your child's *Simply Social Skills Book!*

Here are the **Simply Social 7** for **Being Aware of Your Surroundings**…

❶ **Remove objects that may distract you** – *I will put distracting things away.*

❷ **Don't fool around** – *I will not goof around with my friends.*

❸ **Know your purpose** – *I will think about where I am going and what I am doing.*

❹ **Know who is around you** – *I will be aware of the people around me.*

❺ **Look for potential danger** – *I will look for things that may be unsafe.*

❻ **Listen** – *I will listen to the people and noises around me.*

❼ **Use caution around corners** – *I will slow down when going around corners.*

_____   _____   _____
Parent/Helper Signature   Student Signature   Date

- -

Congratulations!

You are a Simply Social Superstar!

Student Directions: After you return the top of this page to your teacher, cut out the award to the right. Add it to the award page in your *Simply Social Skills Book* or to your award wall in your classroom or at home.

Simply Social 7 — Making Eye Contact

Simply Social 7 Steps

Teacher says: When we talk to others we use more than just our words to communicate. We also communicate with our body language, gestures, and eye contact. *Eye contact* is when we look at a person's eyes as we talk to him/her. We make eye contact with others when we answer questions, share stories, or greet them as we pass in the hallway.

Directions: Teacher will read the **Simply Social 7** steps. Student(s) will read or repeat the statements in italics that follow.

1. **Focus on the other person's face** – If you find it difficult to look directly at someone's eyes, try looking near his/her eyes, like at his/her forehead, nose, or eyebrows.

   I will look at or near people's eyes while talking to them.

2. **Relax!** – When making eye contact, staying relaxed helps you focus on what you are saying to the other person and what he/she is saying to you.

   I will take slow, deep breaths to stay relaxed while making eye contact with others.

3. **Don't stare** – When you look at someone too strongly for too long, it can make him/her feel uncomfortable.

   I will make sure I do not stare at the person I am talking to.

4. **Remember to blink** – One way to avoid staring at someone is by blinking.

   I will remember to blink while I am making eye contact with others.

5. **Glance away from time to time** – When you make eye contact it is natural to look away from time to time. This gives you, and the person you are talking with, a break from looking at each other.

   I will look away from the other person from time to time,
   and then look back at him/her.

6. **Understand that the other person will look away from time to time** – Just as you will not stare at the person you are speaking with, he/she will also glance away and not stare at you.

   I will remember that the person I am talking to will
   look away from me every now and then.

7. **Don't forget to listen!** – As you make eye contact with the person you are speaking with, don't forget to listen! It is just as important to listen to the person you are talking with as it is to look at him/her.

   I know that communicating with others includes both looking AND listening!

 # Making Eye Contact

Look and Learn

Teacher says: The students in this scene are interacting with others in the library.

Directions: 1. **Draw a circle** around each student who **is making eye contact** appropriately.

2. **Draw an X** on each student who **is not making eye contact** appropriately.

Simply Social 7 — Making Eye Contact

Think and Review

Directions: Read the stories, and then answer the questions below about the **Simply Social 7** for **Making Eye Contact**.

1. **In the classroom...** Because Victoria is shy, she has a hard time making eye contact when talking to others. When a classmate asked her a question about the math assignment, Victoria answered while looking at her shoes.

   Did Victoria do the right thing?

   a) Yes – What could she do next?

   b) No – What should she have done?

2. **At school...** Julio is new to his school and couldn't find the art room. When he stopped another student to ask for help, he found it difficult to look directly at her eyes while speaking, so he looked at her nose instead.

   Did Julio do the right thing?

   a) Yes – What could he do next?

   b) No – What should he have done?

3. **At home...** During a conversation with his mom, Brandon was practicing making eye contact. He looked at his mom's eyes, remembered to blink, and glanced away from time to time. He was so busy thinking about what a great job he was doing that he had to ask his mom to repeat what she said!

   Did Brandon do the right thing?

   a) Yes – What could he do next?

   b) No – What should he have done?

4. **In the community...** Lauren was relaxed and focused on the face of her new neighbor while she gave him directions to the local shopping mall.

   Did Lauren do the right thing?

   a) Yes – What could she do next?

   b) No – What should she have done?

Discussion Questions

1. What are some situations in which you had to make eye contact?

2. What would happen if you stared at other people while you talked with them?

 # Making Eye Contact

Take-Home Practice

Dear Parent/Helper,

Today we talked about seven steps to follow when making eye contact called the **Simply Social 7**. Please review these with your child. Have him/her read or repeat the statement in italics that follows each step. Then sign, date, and return this page. We will add this page to your child's *Simply Social Skills Book!*

Here are the **Simply Social 7** for **Making Eye Contact**...

❶ **Focus on the other person's face** – *I will look at or near people's eyes while talking to them.*

❷ **Relax!** – *I will take slow, deep breaths to help me stay relaxed while making eye contact with others.*

❸ **Don't stare** – *I will make sure I do not stare at the person I am talking to.*

❹ **Remember to blink** – *I will remember to blink while I am making eye contact with others.*

❺ **Glance away from time to time** – *I will look away from the other person from time to time, and then look back at him/her.*

❻ **Understand that the other person will look away from time to time** – *I will remember that the person I am talking to will look away from me every now and then.*

❼ **Don't forget to listen!** – *I know that communicating with others includes both looking AND listening!*

_____   _____   _____
Parent/Helper Signature   Student Signature   Date

 -

Congratulations!

You are a Simply Social Superstar!

Student Directions: After you return the top of this page to your teacher, cut out the award to the right. Add it to the award page in your *Simply Social Skills Book* or to your award wall in your classroom or at home.

Using Manners

Simply Social 7 Steps

Teacher says: *Manners* describes the way we behave around others. When we use good manners, we show the people around us that we are polite and that we care about their feelings. Using manners also encourages people to treat us in the same way.

Directions: Teacher will read the **Simply Social 7** steps. Student(s) will read or repeat the statements in italics that follow.

❶ Rudeness is never okay – You are not expected to use your best manners when you're hanging out with your friends, but it is never acceptable to be rude. If you are rude to your friends, they may not want to be friends with you anymore.

I will always treat others with respect.

❷ Remember the Golden Rule – The Golden Rule tells us to treat others in the way that we would want them to treat us.

I will treat people with kindness and respect because that is how I want to be treated.

❸ Say, "Please" and "Thank you" – Always use polite words when talking to people.

I will say, "Please," when I need something and "Thank you," when someone gives me something.

❹ Use your manners when you're eating – When eating with others, remember to use good table manners.

I will chew with my mouth closed and not play with my food or talk with my mouth full.

❺ Respect other people and their property – Don't take things from other people without asking permission first.

I will always ask before using something that does not belong to me.

❻ Use good manners during conversations – Remember that conversations take place between two or more people. Give others an opportunity to speak.

I will take turns being a speaker and a listener, and I will not interrupt if it's not my turn to speak.

❼ Say, "Excuse me" and "I'm sorry" – Think about how your actions affect other people. Use phrases like "excuse me" and "I'm sorry" to correct your actions.

I will say, "Excuse me," if I bump into someone and "I'm sorry," if I hurt someone.

Using Manners

Look and Learn

Teacher says: The students in this scene should be using good manners.

Directions: 1. **Draw a circle** around each student who **is using good manners**.

2. **Draw an X** on each student who **is not using good manners**.

| **Simply Social 7** | **Using Manners** |

Think and Review

Directions: Read the stories, and then answer the questions below about the **Simply Social 7** for **Using Manners**.

1. **In the classroom...** Tyler's classmate was giving a book report to the class. While his classmate was speaking, Tyler asked his friend if he saw the football game over the weekend.

   Did Tyler do the right thing?   a) Yes – What could he do next?

   b) No – What should he have done?

2. **At school...** Millie wanted a drink from the water fountain, but there were two other students standing in her way. Millie pushed past them without saying anything so that she could get a drink

   Did Millie do the right thing?   a) Yes – What could she do next?

   b) No – What should she have done?

3. **At home...** At dinner Tyrone wanted another piece of bread to go with his spaghetti. Tyrone asked his mom if she would please pass the bread.

   Did Tyrone do the right thing?   a) Yes – What could he do next?

   b) No – What should he have done?

4. **In the community...** Janice went to a pizza place with her friends. When her drink was empty she waved her cup in the air and shouted, "Hey you!" to get the server's attention.

   Did Janice do the right thing?   a) Yes – What could she do next?

   b) No – What should she have done?

Discussion Questions

1. What are some situations in which you use manners?

2. What would happen if you were always rude to other people?

Simply Social 7 — Using Manners

Take-Home Practice

Dear Parent/Helper,

Today we talked about seven steps to follow when using manners called the **Simply Social 7**. Please review these with your child. Have him/her read or repeat the statement in italics that follows each step. Then sign, date, and return this page. We will add this page to your child's *Simply Social Skills Book!*

Here are the **Simply Social 7** for **Using Manners**...

1 **Rudeness is never okay** – *I will always treat others with respect.*

2 **Remember the Golden Rule** – *I will treat people with kindness and respect because that is how I want to be treated.*

3 **Say, "Please" and "Thank you"** – *I will say, "Please," when I need something and "Thank you," when someone gives me something.*

4 **Use your manners when you're eating** – *I will chew with my mouth closed and not play with my food or talk with my mouth full.*

5 **Respect other people and their property** – *I will always ask before using something that does not belong to me.*

6 **Use good manners during conversations** – *I will take turns being a speaker and a listener, and I will not interrupt if it's not my turn to speak.*

7 **Say, "Excuse me" and "I'm sorry"** – *I will say, "Excuse me," if I bump into someone and "I'm sorry," if I hurt someone.*

_____   _____   _____
Parent/Helper Signature   Student Signature   Date

- -

Congratulations!

You are a Simply Social Superstar!

Student Directions: After you return the top of this page to your teacher, cut out the award to the right. Add it to the award page in your *Simply Social Skills Book* or to your award wall in your classroom or at home.

Simply Social 7 — Being a Good Listener

Simply Social 7 Steps

Teacher says: When you have something to say, you want others to listen to you. So when someone else is talking, you should be listening to him/her. Part of effective communication is being a good listener. Sometimes it's hard to be a good listener because you may want to be the one talking. However, it is just as important to be a good listener as it is to be a good speaker.

Directions: Teacher will read the **Simply Social 7** steps. Student(s) will read or repeat the statements in italics that follow.

1 **Stop what you're doing** – When someone is talking to you, you should not be doing anything that will distract you from listening to him/her.

I will stop what I am doing so I can focus on the person who is talking.

2 **Pay attention** – Concentrate on understanding the other person's message.

I will focus on what the person speaking to me is saying.

3 **Use good eye contact** – Look at the person who is speaking to you.

I will look at the person who is speaking to me.

4 **Sit or stand still** – Moving around could be distracting to the person who is speaking.

I will not move around or play with my hands or clothing.

5 **Don't interrupt** – You may think of something you want to say while the other person is still speaking, but don't interrupt him/her.

I will wait for a break in the conversation before speaking.

6 **Use responses that show you're listening** – People like to have confirmation that you are listening to them, such as nodding your head when you agree.

I will use simple gestures to show that I am listening.

7 **Don't walk away while the other person is still talking** – It is not polite to walk away from someone while he/she is still speaking.

I will not walk away while the other person is talking.

#BK-371 Simply Social 7™ at School • ©2011 Super Duper® Publications • www.superduperinc.com • 1-800-277-8737

Being a Good Listener

Look and Learn

Teacher says: The students in this scene are involved in conversations in the schoolyard.

Directions: 1. **Draw a circle** around each student who **is being a good listener**.

2. **Draw an X** on each student who **is not being a good listener**.

Simply Social 7 — Being a Good Listener

Think and Review

Directions: Read the stories, and then answer the questions below about the **Simply Social 7** for **Being a Good Listener**.

1. **In the classroom...** Lucas was reading a comic book when his teacher said it was time for the social studies lesson. Lucas put his book away and focused on what his teacher was saying while she presented the lesson.

    Did Lucas do the right thing?   a) Yes – What could he do next?

    b) No – What should he have done?

2. **At school...** Olivia's friend was telling her about an argument she had with her mom. While her friend was talking, Olivia was thinking about what she was going to wear to a party on Saturday.

    Did Olivia do the right thing?   a) Yes – What could she do next?

    b) No – What should she have done?

3. **At home...** Darnell's brother was talking about his school day during dinner. When his brother mentioned that he got an *A* on his English test, Darnell blurted out that he also got an *A* on his spelling test.

    Did Darnell do the right thing?   a) Yes – What could he do next?

    b) No – What should he have done?

4. **In the community...** Chloe asked the clerk in the pet store about the puppies that were for sale. As the clerk was telling her about the puppies, Chloe saw the bunnies in the next aisle and left to go look at them.

    Did Chloe do the right thing?   a) Yes – What could she do next?

    b) No – What should she have done?

Discussion Questions

1. What are some situations in which you had to be a good listener?

2. What would happen if you were talking to someone who wasn't being a good listener?

#BK-371 Simply Social 7™ at School • ©2011 Super Duper® Publications • www.superduperinc.com • 1-800-277-8737

Simply Social 7 — Being a Good Listener

Take-Home Practice

Dear Parent/Helper,

Today we talked about seven steps to follow when being a good listener called the **Simply Social 7**. Please review these with your child. Have him/her read or repeat the statement in italics that follows each step. Then sign, date, and return this page. We will add this page to your child's *Simply Social Skills Book!*

Here are the **Simply Social 7** for **Being a Good Listener**...

1. **Stop what you're doing** – *I will stop what I am doing so I can focus on the person who is talking.*

2. **Pay attention** – *I will focus on what the person speaking to me is saying.*

3. **Use good eye contact** – *I will look at the person who is speaking to me.*

4. **Sit or stand still** – *I will not move around or play with my hands or clothing.*

5. **Don't interrupt** – *I will wait for a break in the conversation before speaking.*

6. **Use responses that show you're listening** – *I will use simple gestures to show that I am listening.*

7. **Don't walk away while the other person is still talking** – *I will not walk away while the other person is talking.*

_____   _____   _____
Parent/Helper Signature   Student Signature   Date

- -

Congratulations!

You are a Simply Social Superstar!

Student Directions: After you return the top of this page to your teacher, cut out the award to the right. Add it to the award page in your *Simply Social Skills Book* or to your award wall in your classroom or at home.

Simply Social 7 — Using an Appropriate Rate of Speech

Simply Social 7 Steps

Teacher says: Your rate of speech is how fast or slow you say your words. Everyone has a different rate of speech depending on his/her location, age, culture, and how he/she feels. In order to communicate effectively we must speak at a rate of speech that our listeners can understand.

Directions: Teacher will read the **Simply Social 7** steps. Student(s) will read or repeat the statements in italics that follow.

1 **Listen to the people around you** – Different people speak at different rates. Listen to find out which rates of speech are easier to understand than others.

*I will listen to others to figure out if a faster
or slower rate of speech is easier to understand.*

2 **Consider your listener's knowledge of the topic** – If your listener is unfamiliar with a topic, you might need to slow your rate of speech to give him/her more time to think about your message.

*I will slow my rate of speech if my listener is unfamiliar
with the subject I am talking about.*

3 **Relax** – If you are nervous about speaking, you may tend to speak at a faster rate than normal.

I will take a deep breath and try to relax so I will not speak too fast.

4 **Use pauses when you speak** – Commas and periods are used to mark breaks in written language. Spoken language should also have breaks. If you speak too fast, try pausing briefly between phrases and sentences.

I will add brief pauses between my phrases and sentences if I speak too fast.

5 **Pay attention to your listener** – Watch and listen to your speaking partner. He/She may be giving you hints that you are speaking too fast or too slow.

I will watch for clues from my listener that tell me I need to adjust my rate of speech.

6 **Practice speaking at different rates of speech** – Using a stopwatch, see how long it takes to read a paragraph at your normal speaking rate. Then practice reading the same paragraph with slower and faster speaking rates.

I will practice using slower and faster speaking rates.

7 **Don't expect your rate of speech to change overnight** – Changing your rate of speech can take time. You have to keep practicing!

I will continue to practice using an appropriate rate of speech.

#BK-371 Simply Social 7™ at School • ©2011 Super Duper® Publications • www.superduperinc.com • 1-800-277-8737

Simply Social 7: Using an Appropriate Rate of Speech

Look and Learn

Teacher says: The students in this scene are talking to other people.

Directions: 1. **Draw a circle** around each student who **is using an appropriate rate of speech**.

2. **Draw an X** on each student who **is not using an appropriate rate of speech**.

Simply Social 7 — Using an Appropriate Rate of Speech

Think and Review

Directions: Read the stories, and then answer the questions below about the **Simply Social 7** for **Using an Appropriate Rate of Speech**.

1. **In the classroom...** Jonathan has a habit of talking too slowly. While speaking to a classmate about an English project, Jonathan noticed that his classmate wasn't paying attention and looked bored. Jonathan started using a faster rate of speech.

   Did Jonathan do the right thing?   a) Yes – What could he do next?

   b) No – What should he have done?

2. **At school...** While waiting for her mom to pick her up from school, Laura was talking to a friend about chess club. Laura knew that her friend didn't play chess, so she slowed her speech rate when talking about the rules for chess.

   Did Laura do the right thing?   a) Yes – What could she do next?

   b) No – What should she have done?

3. **At home...** Samuel and his brother were doing their homework together. When his brother asked him how to solve an addition problem, Samuel explained it quickly. His brother didn't understand what Samuel said and asked him to repeat it. Samuel repeated his explanation just as quickly.

   Did Samuel do the right thing?   a) Yes – What could he do next?

   b) No – What should he have done?

4. **In the community...** While walking down the street, Eliana saw two cars get into an accident. She ran into the nearest store to get help. The store clerk had to keep asking Eliana to repeat herself because she was speaking so fast that the clerk couldn't understand her.

   Did Eliana do the right thing?   a) Yes – What could she do next?

   b) No – What should she have done?

Discussion Questions

1. What are some situations in which you had to adjust your rate of speech?

2. What would happen if the person you were listening to spoke too fast?

#BK-371 Simply Social 7™ at School • ©2011 Super Duper® Publications • www.superduperinc.com • 1-800-277-8737   19

Simply Social 7: Using an Appropriate Rate of Speech

Take-Home Practice

Dear Parent/Helper,

Today we talked about seven steps to follow when using an appropriate rate of speech called the **Simply Social 7**. Please review these with your child. Have him/her read or repeat the statement in italics that follows each step. Then sign, date, and return this page. We will add this page to your child's *Simply Social Skills Book!*

Here are the **Simply Social 7** for **Using an Appropriate Rate of Speech**…

1 **Listen to the people around you** – *I will listen to others to figure out if a faster or slower rate of speech is easier to understand.*

2 **Consider your listener's knowledge of the topic** – *I will slow my rate of speech if my listener is unfamiliar with the subject I am talking about.*

3 **Relax** – *I will take a deep breath and try to relax so I will not speak too fast.*

4 **Use pauses when you speak** – *I will add brief pauses between my phrases and sentences if I speak too fast.*

5 **Pay attention to your listener** – *I will watch for clues from my listener that tell me I need to adjust my rate of speech.*

6 **Practice speaking at different rates of speech** – *I will practice using slower and faster speaking rates.*

7 **Don't expect your rate of speech to change overnight** – *I will continue to practice using an appropriate rate of speech.*

_____   _____   _____
Parent/Helper Signature   Student Signature   Date

- -

Congratulations!

You are a Simply Social Superstar!

Student Directions: After you return the top of this page to your teacher, cut out the award to the right. Add it to the award page in your *Simply Social Skills Book* or to your award wall in your classroom or at home.

Simply Social 7 — Using an Appropriate Volume

Simply Social 7 Steps

Teacher says: *Volume* is the loudness or softness of your voice. If someone is talking too loudly or too softly, it is difficult to concentrate on what he/she is saying. When you are talking to another person it is important to speak at an appropriate volume so that your listener can hear and understand your message.

Directions: Teacher will read the **Simply Social 7** steps. Student(s) will read or repeat the statements in italics that follow.

1 **Know the difference between a soft voice and a loud voice** – Practice using soft and loud voices in order to learn how each one feels and sounds.

I will understand how to use soft and loud voices.

2 **Know your habit** – Many people typically talk too softly or too loudly. If you are aware that you talk softly or loudly, you can adjust your volume to make it easier for a listener to hear you.

I will be aware of my usual volume.

3 **Consider your environment** – The place where you are having a conversation affects how softly or loudly you need to talk. For example, if you are talking to someone in a library, you should use a softer volume than you would use at a football game.

*I will decide how softly or loudly I need to speak by
listening to the noise level of my surroundings.*

4 **Look at the distance between you and your listener** – If you are standing a couple of feet away from your listener, you can speak in a softer voice than if you are standing several yards away.

*I will use a softer voice when my listener is close by and
a louder voice when he/she is farther away.*

5 **Recognize when you are excited about a topic** – When we are excited about a subject, we tend to speak louder and quicker.

*I will monitor my volume to make sure I do not speak too loudly
when I am excited about a subject.*

6 **Watch for nonverbal signals** – Look for signals from your listener that you are speaking too softly or too loudly. For example, if your listener is leaning toward you or asks you to repeat yourself several times, your volume may be too soft. If your listener is backing away or covering his/her ears, you may be speaking too loudly.

I will watch my listener for hints that I am speaking too softly or too loudly.

7 **Adjust your volume** – If you find that your volume is too soft or too loud, change it!

*I will speak louder if I am speaking too softly.
I will speak softer if I am speaking too loudly.*

#BK-371 Simply Social 7™ at School • ©2011 Super Duper® Publications • www.superduperinc.com • 1-800-277-8737

Simply Social 7 — Using an Appropriate Volume

Look and Learn

Teacher says: The students in this scene are performing in the talent show.

Directions: 1. **Draw a circle** around each student who **is using an appropriate volume**.

2. **Draw an X** on each student who **is not using an appropriate volume**.

Simply Social 7 — Using an Appropriate Volume

Think and Review

Directions: Read the stories, and then answer the questions below about the **Simply Social 7** for **Using an Appropriate Volume**.

1. **In the classroom…** During the reading test Hailey's pencil lead broke. Talking in a loud voice, she asked the classmate next to her if she could borrow a pencil.

   Did Hailey do the right thing?   a) Yes – What could she do next?

   b) No – What should she have done?

2. **At school…** Sharon and her friends were talking about the school dance as they walked into the library. As Sharon entered the library she noticed other students looking up at her as she continued to laugh and talk using the same volume she used in the hallway.

   Did Sharon do the right thing?   a) Yes – What could she do next?

   b) No – What should she have done?

3. **At home…** When Christopher arrived home from school he noticed his dad sleeping on the couch. He walked up close to his mom and whispered, "Is Dad sick?"

   Did Christopher do the right thing?   a) Yes – What could he do next?

   b) No – What should he have done?

4. **In the community…** David went to the county fair with a friend. While on the roller coaster David whispered to his friend that it was a fun ride. When his friend asked him to repeat what he said, David whispered again that he thought the ride was fun.

   Did David do the right thing?   a) Yes – What could he do next?

   b) No – What should he have done?

Discussion Questions

1. What are some situations in which you had to adjust your volume level?

2. What would happen if you spoke too softly all of the time?

#BK-371 Simply Social 7™ at School • ©2011 Super Duper® Publications • www.superduperinc.com • 1-800-277-8737   23

Simply Social 7: Using an Appropriate Volume

Take-Home Practice

Dear Parent/Helper,

Today we talked about seven steps to follow when using an appropriate volume called the **Simply Social 7**. Please review these with your child. Have him/her read or repeat the statement in italics that follows each step. Then sign, date, and return this page. We will add this page to your child's *Simply Social Skills Book!*

Here are the **Simply Social 7** for Using an Appropriate Volume…

1. **Know the difference between a soft voice and a loud voice** – *I will understand how to use soft and loud voices.*

2. **Know your habit** – *I will be aware of my usual volume.*

3. **Consider your environment** – *I will decide how softly or loudly I need to speak by listening to the noise level of my surroundings.*

4. **Look at the distance between you and your listener** – *I will use a softer voice when my listener is close by and a louder voice when he/she is farther away.*

5. **Recognize when you are excited about a topic** – *I will monitor my volume to make sure I do not speak too loudly when I am excited about a subject.*

6. **Watch for nonverbal signals** – *I will watch my listener for hints that I am speaking too softly or too loudly.*

7. **Adjust your volume** – *I will speak louder if I am speaking too softly. I will speak softer if I am speaking too loudly.*

_____   _____   _____
Parent/Helper Signature   Student Signature   Date

- -

Congratulations!

You are a Simply Social Superstar!

Student Directions: After you return the top of this page to your teacher, cut out the award to the right. Add it to the award page in your *Simply Social Skills Book* or to your award wall in your classroom or at home.

Simply Social 7 — Respecting Personal Space

Simply Social 7 Steps

Teacher says: *Personal space* is the area immediately surrounding our bodies. Our personal space is our comfort zone. When others invade our personal space it makes us nervous or uncomfortable. Respecting someone's personal space means staying at a distance that helps him/her remain relaxed and calm.

Directions: Teacher will read the **Simply Social 7** steps. Student(s) will read or repeat the statements in italics that follow.

1 **Know how close is too close** – Watch other people to see how far apart they sit or stand from one another. Pay careful attention to their reactions when others invade their personal space.

I will observe others to learn more about personal space.

2 **Stay an arm's length away** – Hold your arm out in front of you. As a general rule, that is the distance you should try to keep between you and another person to avoid getting into his/her personal space.

I will keep a distance of about one arm's length away from the person I am talking to.

3 **Consider how well you know the person** – We are more comfortable when our family members and good friends stand closer to us than when strangers stand closer to us.

I will remember rules about personal space can change depending on how well I know the other person.

4 **Look and see how many other people are around** – Sitting directly beside someone in an empty movie theater is going to seem more threatening than sitting beside someone in a full theater.

I will keep in mind that others may sit or stand closer to each other in crowded areas.

5 **Be careful about touching** – Some people like a hug or a pat on the back every now and then. Others see it as a violation of their personal space and prefer not to be touched.

I will limit hugging or touching people, because it may make them uncomfortable.

6 **Pay attention to others' body language** – If someone backs away from you, you may be standing too close to him/her.

I will remember that other people's reactions let me know when I am in their personal space.

7 **Gently let others know when they have invaded your personal space** – Sometimes others don't know when they have invaded your personal space. It is okay to tell them, but remember to be kind!

If someone invades my personal space, I will take a step back and tell him/her, "I feel more comfortable talking to you at this distance."

#BK-371 Simply Social 7™ at School • ©2011 Super Duper® Publications • www.superduperinc.com • 1-800-277-8737

Simply Social 7 — Respecting Personal Space

Look and Learn

Teacher says: The students in this scene are near other students.

Directions: 1. **Draw a circle** around each student who **is respecting personal space**.

2. **Draw an X** on each student who **is not respecting personal space**.

Simply Social 7 — Respecting Personal Space

Think and Review

Directions: Read the stories, and then answer the questions below about the **Simply Social 7** for **Respecting Personal Space**.

1. **In the classroom...** There was a new student in Destiny's class. Destiny wanted to make him feel welcome, so she walked up to him, stood about six inches away, and introduced herself.

   Did Destiny do the right thing?   a) Yes – What could she do next?

   b) No – What should she have done?

2. **At school...** The cafeteria was almost empty when Adrian walked in with his lunch tray. There were only three other people in the room, and Adrian didn't know any of them. He took his tray to one of the tables and sat two inches away from one of the students.

   Did Adrian do the right thing?   a) Yes – What could he do next?

   b) No – What should he have done?

3. **At home...** Cindy needed some help with her homework. Her dad was in the kitchen, so Cindy went to the kitchen, stood about two feet from her dad, and asked him if he would help her with her homework.

   Did Cindy do the right thing?   a) Yes – What could she do next?

   b) No – What should she have done?

4. **In the community...** Jason's family took him to a new restaurant to celebrate his birthday. When the server brought Jason a free ice cream sundae, Jason thanked the server and gave him a big hug.

   Did Jason do the right thing?   a) Yes – What could he do next?

   b) No – What should he have done?

Discussion Questions

1. What are some situations in which someone sat or stood too close to you?

2. What would happen if there were no consequences for our actions?

Simply Social 7: Respecting Personal Space

Take-Home Practice

Dear Parent/Helper,

Today we talked about seven steps to follow when respecting personal space called the **Simply Social 7**. Please review these with your child. Have him/her read or repeat the statement in italics that follows each step. Then sign, date, and return this page. We will add this page to your child's *Simply Social Skills Book!*

Here are the **Simply Social 7** for **Respecting Personal Space**...

1. **Know how close is too close** – *I will observe others to learn more about personal space.*

2. **Stay an arm's length away** – *I will keep a distance of about one arm's length away from the person I am talking to.*

3. **Consider how well you know the person** – *I will remember rules about personal space can change depending on how well I know the other person.*

4. **Look and see how many other people are around** – *I will keep in mind that others may sit or stand closer to each other in crowded areas.*

5. **Be careful about touching** – *I will limit hugging or touching people, because it may make them uncomfortable.*

6. **Pay attention to others' body language** – *I will remember that other people's reactions let me know when I am in their personal space.*

7. **Gently let others know when they have invaded your personal space** – *If someone invades my personal space, I will take a step back and tell him/her, "I feel more comfortable talking to you at this distance."*

_____   _____   _____
Parent/Helper Signature   Student Signature   Date

- -

Congratulations!

You are a Simply Social Superstar!

Student Directions: After you return the top of this page to your teacher, cut out the award to the right. Add it to the award page in your *Simply Social Skills Book* or to your award wall in your classroom or at home.

Simply Social 7 — Using Greetings

Simply Social 7 Steps

Teacher says: *Greetings* are the words and gestures we use to say hello and goodbye to others. Greetings are an important part of building relationships because they help us connect to other people. When we say, "Hello," it opens the door for communication. When we say, "Goodbye," it signals that the conversation is over for now.

Directions: Teacher will read the **Simply Social 7** steps. Student(s) will read or repeat the statements in italics that follow.

1. **Look at the person you are greeting** – When you look at the person you are speaking to, it helps that person know you are talking to him/her.

   I will look at the person I am greeting.

2. **Be friendly** – If you smile when you greet another person, it starts your conversation on a positive note.

   I will smile and be friendly when I greet people.

3. **Choose your words** – There are several ways to say hello or goodbye. For example, waving, saying, "Hi," "Hello," or "Good afternoon" are all ways to say hello. "Bye," "Goodbye," "So long," and "See you later" are ways to say goodbye.

   I will greet people using the words and gestures that are comfortable for me.

4. **Think about the person you are greeting** – Keep your listener in mind. If you are greeting a teacher or another adult, use a more formal greeting than you would use if greeting your best friend.

   I will use casual greetings with my friends and
   more formal greetings with teachers and other adults.

5. **Say hello when you meet someone** – Whether you know the other person or not, say hello when you meet up with him/her.

   I will say hello when I cross paths with someone.

6. **Respond to someone else's greeting** – If someone says hello or goodbye to you, respond with a similar greeting of your own.

   I will say, "Hi!" when someone says hello to me
   and "Bye!" when someone says goodbye to me.

7. **Say goodbye when you leave** – When you are finished speaking to someone, say goodbye to let him/her know that your current conversation is over.

   I will say goodbye to the person I'm speaking to when I am ready to leave.

#BK-371 Simply Social 7™ at School • ©2011 Super Duper® Publications • www.superduperinc.com • 1-800-277-8737

29

Using Greetings

Look and Learn

Teacher says: The students in this scene are using greetings.

Directions: 1. **Draw a circle** around each student who **is using an appropriate greetings**.

2. **Draw an X** on each student who **is not using an appropriate greetings**.

Simply Social 7 — Using Greetings

Think and Review

Directions: Read the stories, and then answer the questions below about the **Simply Social 7** for **Using Greetings**.

1. **In the classroom...** When Samantha arrived at her morning class, her teacher, Ms. Hanson, was standing by the door. Samantha looked at her teacher and said, "Good morning, Ms. Hanson!"

   Did Samantha do the right thing?   a) Yes – What could she do next?

   b) No – What should she have done?

2. **At school...** On his way to the library Anthony saw his principal in the lobby. As he passed by he said to his principal, "Hey, dude! What's up?"

   Did Anthony do the right thing?   a) Yes – What could he do next?

   b) No – What should he have done?

3. **At home...** When Alexis came home from school her little brother met her at the door and told her, "Hi! I'm glad you're home!" Alexis pushed past him and asked her mom for a snack.

   Did Alexis do the right thing?   a) Yes – What could she do next?

   b) No – What should she have done?

4. **In the community...** While walking down the sidewalk Aaron saw a boy coming toward him. Aaron looked at the boy and when the boy looked back, Aaron said hello to him.

   Did Aaron do the right thing?   a) Yes – What could he do next?

   b) No – What should he have done?

Discussion Questions

1. What are some situations in which you use greetings?

2. What would happen if you never looked at others while greeting them?

#BK-371 Simply Social 7™ at School • ©2011 Super Duper® Publications • www.superduperinc.com • 1-800-277-8737

Simply Social 7: Using Greetings

Take-Home Practice

Dear Parent/Helper,

Today we talked about seven steps to follow when using greetings called the **Simply Social 7**. Please review these with your child. Have him/her read or repeat the statement in italics that follows each step. Then sign, date, and return this page. We will add this page to your child's *Simply Social Skills Book!*

Here are the **Simply Social 7** for **Using Greetings**…

❶ **Look at the person you are greeting** – *I will look at the person I am greeting.*

❷ **Be friendly** – *I will smile and be friendly when I greet people.*

❸ **Choose your words** – *I will greet people using the words and gestures that are comfortable for me.*

❹ **Think about the person you are greeting** – *I will use casual greetings with my friends and more formal greetings with teachers and other adults.*

❺ **Say hello when you meet someone** – *I will say hello when I cross paths with someone.*

❻ **Respond to someone else's greeting** – *I will say, "Hi!" when someone says hello to me and "Bye!" when someone says goodbye to me.*

❼ **Say goodbye when you leave** – *I will say goodbye to the person I'm speaking to when I am ready to leave.*

_____   _____   _____
Parent/Helper Signature   Student Signature   Date

Congratulations!

You are a Simply Social Superstar!

Student Directions: After you return the top of this page to your teacher, cut out the award to the right. Add it to the award page in your *Simply Social Skills Book* or to your award wall in your classroom or at home.

32   #BK-371 Simply Social 7™ at School   •   ©2011 Super Duper® Publications   •   www.superduperinc.com   •   1-800-277-8737

Simply Social 7™

Starting a Conversation

Simply Social 7 Steps

Teacher says: When people talk back and forth sharing their ideas, thoughts, or feelings, they are having a *conversation*. Conversations are important because they help us get to know each other better. During conversations, we learn what other people like, dislike, and how they feel about certain subjects. Starting a conversation can be tricky, but it is a skill you can learn with practice.

Directions: Teacher will read the **Simply Social 7** steps. Student(s) will read or repeat the statements in italics that follow.

1 **Relax** – It is easier to talk to other people when you are relaxed.

I will take a deep breath to help myself relax
if I am nervous about starting a conversation.

2 **Approach the other person** – You cannot have a conversation at a distance. In order to have a conversation, you must walk up to the other person.

I will walk up to the person I want to have a conversation with.

3 **Smile and greet the other person** – When you approach someone to start a conversation, smile and say hello.

I will smile and say, "Hi!" to begin a conversation.

4 **Ask the other person how he/she is doing** – Greetings are often followed with a question about the other person's well-being, such as "How's it going?" or "How are you?"

I will ask the other person, "How are you today?"

5 **Make small talk** – Small talk is light conversation about common things such as music, sports, hobbies, or school. These are good topics to start a conversation with.

I will start a conversation by talking about music, sports, hobbies, or school.

6 **Be yourself** – You don't have to pretend to like something just to keep the conversation going. There are plenty of other things to talk about. Keep making small talk until you find something you both enjoy talking about.

I will act naturally and talk about subjects that interest both of us.

7 **Pay attention** – If you listen to the other person, you might hear something you can continue to talk about.

I will listen to the other person and comment on the things he/she says.

#BK-371 Simply Social 7™ at School • ©2011 Super Duper® Publications • www.superduperinc.com • 1-800-277-8737   33

Starting a Conversation

Look and Learn

Teacher says: The students in this scene are starting conversations.

Directions: 1. **Draw a circle** around each student who **is starting a conversation** appropriately.

2. **Draw an X** on each student who **is not starting a conversation** appropriately.

Simply Social 7™

Starting a Conversation

Think and Review

Directions: Read the stories, and then answer the questions below about the **Simply Social 7** for **Starting a Conversation**.

1. **In the classroom...** Marisol wanted to start a conversation with the new student in her class. After introducing herself and making small talk, Marisol found out that the new student spoke French. Marisol told the new student that she also spoke French, even though she did not.

   Did Marisol do the right thing?   a) Yes – What could she do next?

   b) No – What should she have done?

2. **At school...** Angie was waiting in line at the water fountain and decided to start a conversation with the person behind her. She turned around and said, "I like fairies."

   Did Angie do the right thing?   a) Yes – What could she do next?

   b) No – What should she have done?

3. **At home...** Julian wanted to talk to his brother about the game that was about to start on television. He walked up to his brother and said, "Hi! How was your day?"

   Did Julian do the right thing?   a) Yes – What could he do next?

   b) No – What should he have done?

4. **In the community...** While walking his dog through the neighborhood, Corey saw his friend who was standing four houses away. Corey shouted, "Hey! How's it going?"

   Did Corey do the right thing?   a) Yes – What could he do next?

   b) No – What should he have done?

Discussion Questions

1. What are some situations in which you wanted to start a conversation?

2. What would happen if no one ever approached anyone else to start a conversation?

#BK-371 Simply Social 7™ at School • ©2011 Super Duper® Publications • www.superduperinc.com • 1-800-277-8737

Simply Social 7 — Starting a Conversation

Take-Home Practice

Dear Parent/Helper,

Today we talked about seven steps to follow when starting a conversation called the **Simply Social 7**. Please review these with your child. Have him/her read or repeat the statement in italics that follows each step. Then sign, date, and return this page. We will add this page to your child's *Simply Social Skills Book!*

Here are the **Simply Social 7** for **Starting a Conversation**…

❶ **Relax** – *I will take a deep breath to help myself relax if I am nervous about starting a conversation.*

❷ **Approach the other person** – *I will walk up to the person I want to have a conversation with.*

❸ **Smile and greet the other person** – *I will smile and say, "Hi!" to begin a conversation.*

❹ **Ask the other person how he/she is doing** – *I will ask the other person, "How are you today?"*

❺ **Make small talk** – *I will start a conversation by talking about music, sports, hobbies, or school.*

❻ **Be yourself** – *I will act naturally and talk about subjects that interest both of us.*

❼ **Pay attention** – *I will listen to the other person and comment on the things he/she says.*

_____   _____   _____
Parent/Helper Signature   Student Signature   Date

 -

Congratulations!

You are a Simply Social Superstar!

Student Directions: After you return the top of this page to your teacher, cut out the award to the right. Add it to the award page in your *Simply Social Skills Book* or to your award wall in your classroom or at home.

36   #BK-371 Simply Social 7™ at School   •   ©2011 Super Duper® Publications   •   www.superduperinc.com   •   1-800-277-8737

Simply Social 7™
Joining a Conversation

Simply Social 7 Steps

Teacher says: A *conversation* is when two or more people take turns talking and sharing their thoughts, ideas, or opinions. Sometimes you might want to say something related to the conversation. In order to share your opinion or ask a question about the subject of the conversation, you will have to join the conversation.

Directions: Teacher will read the **Simply Social 7** steps. Student(s) will read or repeat the statements in italics that follow.

1 **Don't try to join private conversations** – If others are discussing something that might be considered personal, or if they are whispering or talking very quietly to one another, stay out of the conversation.

I will remember that if people are speaking quietly to one another, they may be discussing personal matters that are none of my business.

2 **Listen to the topic** – Before trying to join a conversation, make sure you know what others are talking about.

I will listen to what other people are saying in order to learn what the conversation is about.

3 **Don't speak unless you have something to say about the subject** – Decide whether or not you have anything to contribute about the subject of conversation.

I will not join the conversation unless I have a question or comment about the subject.

4 **Watch your body language** – When joining conversations, your body language should be pleasant and friendly.

I will relax and keep a pleasant look on my face when joining a conversation.

5 **Keep your comments positive and polite** – Remember you want to participate in a conversation that other people are already involved in. Don't be negative or aggressive.

I will remain pleasant and considerate when I join someone else's conversation.

6 **Start with a small comment and judge others' reactions** – If you make a comment about the conversation and others don't seem to mind, feel free to stay with the group and their conversation. If other people react negatively, apologize for interrupting and remain quiet or move to a different group.

I will comment on something that someone said and use others' reactions to determine if I should continue to participate in the conversation.

7 **Make relevant remarks** – Keep your remarks on topic. Don't try to dominate the conversation or change the subject.

I will share comments and ask questions related to the subject that others are talking about.

#BK-371 Simply Social 7™ at School • ©2011 Super Duper® Publications • www.superduperinc.com • 1-800-277-8737

37

Joining a Conversation

Look and Learn

Teacher says: The students in this scene are joining others' conversations.

Directions: 1. **Draw a circle** around each student who **is joining a conversation** appropriately.

2. **Draw an X** on each student who **is not joining a conversation** appropriately.

Simply Social 7™
Joining a Conversation

Think and Review

Directions: Read the stories, and then answer the questions below about the **Simply Social 7** for **Joining a Conversation**.

1. **In the classroom...** Two of Julia's classmates were whispering quietly to each other. Julia approached her classmates and asked, "What are you talking about?" When her classmates didn't respond, Julia repeated the question.

   Did Julia do the right thing?   a) Yes – What could she do next?

   b) No – What should she have done?

2. **At school...** At recess Zachary was listening to his friends talk about football. One of his friends said Florida State would win the championship this season. Zachary commented, "They have a good team this year!" Zachary's friend agreed and asked Zachary which college team was his favorite.

   Did Zachary do the right thing?   a) Yes – What could he do next?

   b) No – What should he have done?

3. **At home...** Tiara's mom and dad were talking about where they should put the new piano. Tiara listened for a while, then agreed with her mom that the new piano would look great in front of the window.

   Did Tiara do the right thing?   a) Yes – What could she do next?

   b) No – What should she have done?

4. **In the community...** Jordan went to the grocery store to get a gallon of milk for his mom. While walking past the bread he saw two girls talking in the aisle. As Jordan passed the girls he said, "Wheat bread is gross!"

   Did Jordan do the right thing?   a) Yes – What could he do next?

   b) No – What should he have done?

Discussion Questions

1. What are some situations in which you wanted to join a conversation?

2. What would happen if you made a comment during a conversation without listening to the topic first?

#BK-371 Simply Social 7™ at School • ©2011 Super Duper® Publications • www.superduperinc.com • 1-800-277-8737   39

Simply Social 7: Joining a Conversation

Take-Home Practice

Dear Parent/Helper,

Today we talked about seven steps to follow when joining a conversation called the **Simply Social 7**. Please review these with your child. Have him/her read or repeat the statement in italics that follows each step. Then sign, date, and return this page. We will add this page to your child's *Simply Social Skills Book!*

Here are the **Simply Social 7** for **Joining a Conversation**…

1. **Don't try to join private conversations** – *I will remember that if people are speaking quietly to one another, they may be discussing personal matters that are none of my business.*

2. **Listen to the topic** – *I will listen to what other people are saying in order to learn what the conversation is about.*

3. **Don't speak unless you have something to say about the subject** – *I will not join the conversation unless I have a question or comment about the subject.*

4. **Watch your body language** – *I will relax and keep a pleasant look on my face when joining a conversation.*

5. **Keep your comments positive and polite** – *I will remain pleasant and considerate when I join someone else's conversation.*

6. **Start with a small comment and judge others' reactions** – *I will comment on something that someone said and use others' reactions to determine if I should continue to participate in the conversation.*

7. **Make relevant remarks** – *I will share comments and ask questions related to the subject that others are talking about.*

_____   _____   _____
Parent/Helper Signature   Student Signature   Date

- -

Congratulations!

You are a Simply Social Superstar!

Student Directions: After you return the top of this page to your teacher, cut out the award to the right. Add it to the award page in your *Simply Social Skills Book* or to your award wall in your classroom or at home.

40   #BK-371 Simply Social 7™ at School   •   ©2011 Super Duper® Publications   •   www.superduperinc.com   •   1-800-277-8737

Simply Social 7 — Expressing Opinions

Simply Social 7 Steps

Teacher says: Everybody has opinions. When you share what you believe or feel about something you are expressing your *opinion*. Opinions are not right or wrong. They help other people understand what you like and dislike or what you think about certain topics.

Directions: Teacher will read the **Simply Social 7** steps. Student(s) will read or repeat the statements in italics that follow.

1 Listen – Listen to the topic being discussed. You can't express your opinion about a topic if you don't know what the topic is.

I will pay attention to what other people are talking about
so that my opinion will be on topic.

2 Don't be afraid to share your opinion – Everybody has opinions. Don't be afraid to express yours.

I will remember that opinions are not right or wrong,
so I will not be afraid to share what I think.

3 Use words that let listeners know you're giving your opinion – When giving your opinion, use words such as "I think...," "In my opinion...," or "I believe..." to alert your listener that you are about to give your opinion.

I will use words that let my listeners know I am expressing my opinion.

4 Stay on topic and state your opinion clearly – Your opinion should relate to the topic that is being discussed and should be said in a clear way that your listener can understand.

I will be specific and stay on topic when giving my opinion.

5 Be kind – Don't give opinions that are hurtful and don't laugh at others because of their opinions.

I will be kind when expressing my opinions
and when commenting on the opinions of others.

6 Listen to others' opinions – Give other people the opportunity to express their opinions.

I will listen and be polite when others are sharing their opinions.

7 Keep an open mind – Don't make up your mind in advance that someone else's opinion isn't as good as yours.

I will listen to someone else's opinion before I make a judgment.

#BK-371 Simply Social 7™ at School • ©2011 Super Duper® Publications • www.superduperinc.com • 1-800-277-8737

Expressing Opinions

Look and Learn

Teacher says: The students in this scene are expressing their opinions on different topics.

Directions: 1. **Draw a circle** around each student who **is expressing opinions** appropriately.

2. **Draw an X** on each student who **is not expressing opinions** appropriately.

Simply Social 7™

Expressing Opinions

Think and Review

Directions: Read the stories, and then answer the questions below about the **Simply Social 7** for **Expressing Opinions**.

1. **In the classroom...** Malik's class was having a debate about whether or not there should be rules about the kinds of food served in the cafeteria. Malik told the class, "I think it is a good idea because it will give students healthier lunch choices!"

   Did Malik do the right thing?   a) Yes – What could he do next?

   b) No – What should he have done?

2. **At school...** During basketball practice Claire's friend said she thought Kareem Abdul-Jabbar was the greatest basketball player ever. Claire said, "You're wrong! Charles Barkley is the best player ever!"

   Did Claire do the right thing?   a) Yes – What could she do next?

   b) No – What should she have done?

3. **At home...** Luke's mom spent several hours in the kitchen making dinner. At dinner time Luke took a bite of his meatloaf and told his mom, "This meatloaf is terrible! It tastes like dog food!"

   Did Luke do the right thing?   a) Yes – What could he do next?

   b) No – What should he have done?

4. **In the community...** Selena's sister needed a haircut, so Selena went with her to the salon. When the hair stylist was finished with the haircut, Selena said to her sister, "That's the goofiest haircut I've ever seen!"

   Did Selena do the right thing?   a) Yes – What could she do next?

   b) No – What should she have done?

Discussion Questions

1. What are some situations in which you had to express your opinions?

2. What would happen if you disagreed with someone else's opinion?

#BK-371 Simply Social 7™ at School • ©2011 Super Duper® Publications • www.superduperinc.com • 1-800-277-8737

Simply Social 7 — Expressing Opinions

Take-Home Practice

Dear Parent/Helper,

Today we talked about seven steps to follow when expressing opinions called the **Simply Social 7**. Please review these with your child. Have him/her read or repeat the statement in italics that follows each step. Then sign, date, and return this page. We will add this page to your child's *Simply Social Skills Book!*

Here are the **Simply Social 7** for **Expressing Opinions**...

❶ **Listen** – *I will pay attention to what other people are talking about so that my opinion will be on topic.*

❷ **Don't be afraid to share your opinion** – *I will remember that opinions are not right or wrong, so I will not be afraid to share what I think.*

❸ **Use words that let listeners know you're giving your opinion** – *I will use words that let my listeners know I am expressing my opinion.*

❹ **Stay on topic and state your opinion clearly** – *I will be specific and stay on topic when giving my opinion.*

❺ **Be kind** – *I will be kind when expressing my opinions and when commenting on the opinions of others.*

❻ **Listen to others' opinions** – *I will listen and be polite when others are sharing their opinions.*

❼ **Keep an open mind** – *I will listen to someone else's opinion before I make a judgment.*

_____   _____   _____
Parent/Helper Signature   Student Signature   Date

Congratulations!

You are a Simply Social Superstar!

Student Directions: After you return the top of this page to your teacher, cut out the award to the right. Add it to the award page in your *Simply Social Skills Book* or to your award wall in your classroom or at home.

Simply Social 7 — Giving Enough Information

Simply Social 7 Steps

Teacher says: "We went somewhere the other day and that guy gave me a thing that does something and…" Have you ever been in a conversation like this? It's hard to follow a conversation when the person you're talking to doesn't give you enough information to understand what is going on.

Directions: Teacher will read the **Simply Social 7** steps. Student(s) will read or repeat the statements in italics that follow.

1 **Keep in mind how well you know your listener** – If you haven't spent a lot of time talking and interacting with your listener, he/she is less likely to know about your topic and will probably need more information than someone you speak to often.

I will keep in mind how much time I spend with my listener.

2 **Think about what your listener knows** – If your listener is not familiar with your topic of conversation, you will need to give him/her more information about it. A listener who knows a lot about the topic will need less information.

I will determine how much my listener knows about the topic.

3 **Consider whether you have talked about it before** – If you have never talked about the subject with your listener before, then he/she might need more information.

I will give my listener more information if I have not talked to him/her about the topic before.

4 **Start with the basics** – Make sure you have told your listener the basic information he/she will need to understand what you are talking about.

I will tell my listener the who, what, when, and where about my topic.

5 **Don't give unnecessary information** – Don't confuse your listener with extra information that he/she doesn't need to know in order to understand what you are talking about.

I will only give my listener the information he/she needs to understand what I am talking about.

6 **Watch your listener** – Your listener's body language can tell you if he/she has enough information to follow and understand your topic of conversation.

I will watch to see if my listener looks confused because I have not given him/her enough information.

7 **Listen to your conversational partner** – Your listener's verbal responses will also tell you if he/she has enough information to follow and understand your topic of conversation.

I will listen to my partner's responses that may indicate I am not giving him/her enough information.

#BK-371 Simply Social 7™ at School • ©2011 Super Duper® Publications • www.superduperinc.com • 1-800-277-8737

45

Simply Social 7: Giving Enough Information

Look and Learn

Teacher says: The students in this scene are talking to other students.

Directions: 1. **Draw a circle** around each student who **is giving enough information**.

2. **Draw an X** on each student who **is not giving enough information**.

Simply Social 7™ — Giving Enough Information

Think and Review

Directions: Read the stories, and then answer the questions below about the **Simply Social 7** for **Giving Enough Information.**

1. **In the classroom…** Teresa was telling her classmate about a birthday party she went to but didn't say who the party was for. When her classmate asked who the party was for, Teresa got mad and said her classmate wasn't listening.

   Did Teresa do the right thing?　　　a) Yes – What could she do next?

   　　　　　　　　　　　　　　　　　b) No – What should she have done?

2. **At school…** Frank told his football team that they were going to practice the play that won them the championship game last year. Frank forgot that they had a new player this year and didn't explain the play.

   Did Frank do the right thing?　　　a) Yes – What could he do next?

   　　　　　　　　　　　　　　　　b) No – What should he have done?

3. **At home…** Mary was telling her mom about the pizza party her class won. She told her mom when the party was, what kind of pizza they had, and that they won the party for collecting the most cans of food during the food drive.

   Did Mary do the right thing?　　　a) Yes – What could she do next?

   　　　　　　　　　　　　　　　　b) No – What should she have done?

4. **In the community…** Pedro saw two teenagers painting graffiti on the side of a building. When the police arrived, Pedro gave the officers a description of the teenagers. Based on Pedro's description, the police were able to find the teenagers involved in the vandalism.

   Did Pedro do the right thing?　　　a) Yes – What could he do next?

   　　　　　　　　　　　　　　　　b) No – What should he have done?

Discussion Questions

1. What are some situations in which you gave enough information?

2. What would happen if you left out important details when speaking to someone?

#BK-371 Simply Social 7™ at School • ©2011 Super Duper® Publications • www.superduperinc.com • 1-800-277-8737

Simply Social 7: Giving Enough Information

Take-Home Practice

Dear Parent/Helper,

Today we talked about seven steps to follow when giving enough information called the **Simply Social 7**. Please review these with your child. Have him/her read or repeat the statement in italics that follows each step. Then sign, date, and return this page. We will add this page to your child's *Simply Social Skills Book!*

Here are the **Simply Social 7** for **Giving Enough Information**…

1. **Keep in mind how well you know your listener** – *I will keep in mind how much time I spend with my listener.*

2. **Think about what your listener knows** – *I will determine how much my listener knows about the topic.*

3. **Consider whether you have talked about it before** – *I will give my listener more information if I haven't talked to him/her about the topic before.*

4. **Start with the basics** – *I will tell my listener the* who, what, when, *and* where *about my topic.*

5. **Don't give unnecessary information** – *I will only give my listener the information he/she needs to understand what I am talking about.*

6. **Watch your listener** – *I will watch to see if my listener looks confused because I have not given him/her enough information.*

7. **Listen to your conversational partner** – *I will listen to my partner's responses that may indicate I am not giving him/her enough information.*

_____   _____   _____
Parent/Helper Signature   Student Signature   Date

- -

Congratulations!

You are a Simply Social Superstar!

Student Directions: After you return the top of this page to your teacher, cut out the award to the right. Add it to the award page in your *Simply Social Skills Book* or to your award wall in your classroom or at home.

Simply Social 7 — Asking for More Information

Simply Social 7 Steps

Teacher says: Sometimes when another person is speaking, you might not understand what he/she is talking about. You might be afraid to ask questions because other people in the group seem to understand. When your teacher is speaking it is important to understand what he/she is talking about. If your teacher says something you don't understand, you should ask for more information.

Directions: Teacher will read the **Simply Social 7** steps. Student(s) will read or repeat the statements in italics that follow.

1 Get the speaker's attention – If someone says something you don't understand, politely get his/her attention so you can ask for more information.

I will raise my hand or politely say "Excuse me" to get the speaker's attention. Then I will wait to be called on before I continue speaking.

2 Ask politely – Choose words that help you ask polite questions.

I will use polite words like, "Could you please tell me…?" or "Would you mind explaining…?"

3 Give an explanation – Tell the speaker exactly what you do not understand.

I will use explanations such as, "I don't know what you meant by…" or "I'm not sure what that means."

4 Ask if the information can be given in a different way – If you don't understand the speaker's vocabulary, ask him/her to tell you the same information using different words.

I will ask the speaker to give the information in a different way if I do not understand it.

5 Request more details – If you have a general idea of what the speaker is talking about but would like to understand better, you can ask for more details.

I will ask the speaker to give me more details if I want to understand the topic better.

6 Ask for an example – Sometimes it's easier to understand what someone is talking about if he/she gives you an example.

I will ask the speaker to give me an example of what he/she is talking about.

7 Restate what you think the person said – To make sure you understand what the person is talking about, try repeating it back to him/her. Then the speaker will either confirm that you are right or try to explain it to you in another way.

I will repeat back to the speaker what I think he/she said.

#BK-371 Simply Social 7™ at School • ©2011 Super Duper® Publications • www.superduperinc.com • 1-800-277-8737

Simply Social 7 — Asking for More Information

Look and Learn

Teacher says: The students in this scene would like more information about lacrosse.

Directions: 1. **Draw a circle** around each student who **is asking for more information** appropriately.

2. **Draw an X** on each student who **is not asking for more information** appropriately.

Simply Social 7™ — Asking for More Information

Think and Review

Directions: Read the stories, and then answer the questions below about the **Simply Social 7** for **Asking for More Information**.

1. **In the classroom...** Lily's teacher told the class to put their homework assignments in the homework holder. Lily is new to the class and didn't understand what the teacher meant, so she asked for more information.

   Did Lily do the right thing?   a) Yes – What could she do next?

   b) No – What should she have done?

2. **At school...** Addison joined the robotics team at his school. During one of the meetings someone was talking about using a phototropic sensor. Addison didn't know what that was, so he asked for an explanation.

   Did Addison do the right thing?   a) Yes – What could he do next?

   b) No – What should he have done?

3. **At home...** Saria was helping her dad in the garage. Her dad asked her to hand him a tool that she was not familiar with. So Saria took a guess and handed him the wrong tool.

   Did Saria do the right thing?   a) Yes – What could she do next?

   b) No – What should she have done?

4. **In the community...** A sign posted at the entrance of a public restroom said the restroom was closed for maintenance. Michael wasn't sure what that meant, so he pushed past an employee to get into the restroom.

   Did Michael do the right thing?   a) Yes – What could he do next?

   b) No – What should he have done?

Discussion Questions

1. What are some situations in which you had to ask for more information?

2. What would happen if you didn't understand something your teacher said and you didn't ask for more information?

#BK-371 Simply Social 7™ at School • ©2011 Super Duper® Publications • www.superduperinc.com • 1-800-277-8737   51

Simply Social 7: Asking for More Information

Take-Home Practice

Dear Parent/Helper,

Today we talked about seven steps to follow when asking for more information called the **Simply Social 7**. Please review these with your child. Have him/her read or repeat the statement in italics that follows each step. Then sign, date, and return this page. We will add this page to your child's *Simply Social Skills Book!*

Here are the **Simply Social 7** for **Asking for More Information**…

1. **Get the speaker's attention** – *I will raise my hand or politely say, "Excuse me" to get the speaker's attention. Then I will wait to be called on before I continue speaking.*

2. **Ask politely** – *I will use polite words like, "Could you please tell me…?" or "Would you mind explaining…?"*

3. **Give an explanation** – *I will use explanations such as "I don't know what you meant by…" or "I'm not sure what that means."*

4. **Ask if the information can be given in a different way** – *I will ask the speaker to give the information in a different way if I do not understand it.*

5. **Request more details** – *I will ask the speaker to give me more details if I want to understand the topic better.*

6. **Ask for an example** – *I will ask the speaker to give me an example of what he/she is talking about.*

7. **Restate what you think the person said** – *I will repeat back to the speaker what I think he/she said.*

_____   _____   _____
Parent/Helper Signature   Student Signature   Date

- -

Congratulations!

You are a Simply Social Superstar!

Student Directions: After you return the top of this page to your teacher, cut out the award to the right. Add it to the award page in your *Simply Social Skills Book* or to your award wall in your classroom or at home.

Staying on Topic

Simply Social 7 Steps

Teacher says: During a conversation individuals take turns sharing their thoughts and opinions about a topic. It is important to stay on topic so everyone can follow along and participate. If the topic of conversation changes too many times or too quickly, the conversation becomes difficult to follow.

Directions: Teacher will read the **Simply Social 7** steps. Student(s) will read or repeat the statements in italics that follow.

❶ Know the topic before speaking – Before participating in a conversation, make sure you understand what the topic of conversation is.

I will make sure I know what others are talking about before I join a conversation.

❷ Ask questions to learn about the topic – One way to participate in the conversation and stay on topic is to ask questions to learn more about the current topic.

I will stay on topic and get more information about it by asking questions.

❸ Use comments and non-verbal gestures to show you are listening – Nodding your head, agreeing with comments, and making eye contact are all ways to show you are listening and following the topic of conversation.

I will use responses such as nodding my head, agreeing with others, and making eye contact to show I am following the conversation.

❹ Add information about the topic to the conversation – Conversations require people to take turns speaking and listening. Share what you know about the topic with the others involved in the conversation.

I will share what I know about the topic.

❺ Let everyone have a chance to talk – Let everyone have a chance to give information, ask questions, or comment about the current topic.

I will not dominate the topic and will let everyone have the opportunity to talk about it.

❻ Wait to talk about unrelated topics – If you have something to say that is not about the current topic, wait until everyone is finished talking before you introduce a new topic.

I will not make comments that are off topic.

❼ Practice identifying others' off-topic remarks – While participating in conversations, listen to others' comments. Try to decide if their comments are about the topic or if they are off topic.

I will listen to the comments made by other people and judge whether or not they are about the topic.

#BK-371 Simply Social 7™ at School • ©2011 Super Duper® Publications • www.superduperinc.com • 1-800-277-8737

53

Staying on Topic

Look and Learn

Teacher says: The students in this scene are having conversations with each other.

Directions: 1. **Draw a circle** around each student who **is staying on topic**.

2. **Draw an X** on each student who **is not staying on topic**.

Simply Social 7 — Staying on Topic

Think and Review

Directions: Read the stories, and then answer the questions below about the **Simply Social 7** for **Staying on Topic**.

1. **In the classroom...** Alejandro's class was learning about pilgrims. Since Alejandro used to live in Massachusetts and had seen many museum exhibits about pilgrims, he shared what he knew about pilgrims.

   Did Alejandro do the right thing?   a) Yes – What could he do next?

                                                          b) No – What should he have done?

2. **At school...** During swim team practice Chelsea's friends were talking about a new movie that just came out. Chelsea hadn't seen the movie, so she asked her friends, "What do you think about the new lunch menu?"

   Did Chelsea do the right thing?   a) Yes – What could she do next?

                                                          b) No – What should she have done?

3. **At home...** Hope was talking to her sister about their upcoming shopping trip. When Hope's sister said she wanted to buy new shoes, it reminded Hope that she wanted to borrow her sister's new skirt. Hope asked her sister, "Where do you want to shop for new shoes?"

   Did Hope do the right thing?   a) Yes – What could she do next?

                                                          b) No – What should she have done?

4. **In the community...** Miles ran into some of his friends at the mall. He could see his friends were in the middle of a conversation, but he didn't know what they were talking about. As soon as Miles joined the group he asked if any of them had been to the new toy store.

   Did Miles do the right thing?   a) Yes – What could he do next?

                                                          b) No – What should he have done?

Discussion Questions

1. What are some situations in which you had to stay on topic?

2. What would happen if the person you were talking to changed topics every time he/she spoke?

#BK-371 Simply Social 7™ at School • ©2011 Super Duper® Publications • www.superduperinc.com • 1-800-277-8737   55

Simply Social 7: Staying on Topic

Take-Home Practice

Dear Parent/Helper,

Today we talked about seven steps to follow when staying on topic called the **Simply Social 7**. Please review these with your child. Have him/her read or repeat the statement in italics that follows each step. Then sign, date, and return this page. We will add this page to your child's *Simply Social Skills Book!*

Here are the **Simply Social 7** for **Staying on Topic**...

1. **Know the topic before speaking** – *I will make sure I know what others are talking about before I join a conversation.*

2. **Ask questions to learn about the topic** – *I will stay on topic and get more information about it by asking questions.*

3. **Use comments and non-verbal gestures to show you are listening** – *I will use responses such as nodding my head, agreeing with others, and making eye contact to show I am following the conversation.*

4. **Add information about the topic to the conversation** – *I will share what I know about the topic.*

5. **Let everyone have a chance to talk** – *I will not dominate the topic and will let everyone have the opportunity to talk about it.*

6. **Wait to talk about unrelated topics** – *I will not make comments that are off topic.*

7. **Practice identifying others' off-topic remarks** – *I will listen to the comments made by other people and judge whether or not they are about the topic.*

_____   _____   _____
Parent/Helper Signature   Student Signature   Date

- -

Congratulations!

You are a Simply Social Superstar!

Student Directions: After you return the top of this page to your teacher, cut out the award to the right. Add it to the award page in your *Simply Social Skills Book* or to your award wall in your classroom or at home.

Switching Topics

Simply Social 7 Steps

Teacher says: It is important to know when and how to switch topics in a conversation. If you change topics too quickly, others will get confused. If you wait too long to change a topic, others will lose interest in the conversation.

Directions: Teacher will read the **Simply Social 7** steps. Student(s) will read or repeat the statements in italics that follow.

❶ Pay attention – Listen to the current topic of conversation, so you will know when it is time to change topics.

I will pay attention to what others are saying so I will recognize when it is okay to switch topics.

❷ Don't change topics if others are still interested in the current topic – If other people are still talking about the subject and appear to be interested, wait to switch topics.

I will stay on the topic of conversation if others are still interested in it.

❸ Recognize the signals – When there are breaks in the conversation, or if others are checking their watches, looking bored, or moving around restlessly, it may be time to introduce a new topic.

I will watch for non-verbal signals to know when to introduce a new topic.

❹ Wait for a pause in the conversation – Remember it's impolite to interrupt another person, so don't interrupt someone else to switch topics. Wait until there is a break before suggesting a new topic.

I will wait for a break in the conversation to switch topics.

❺ Don't change topics without warning – If you change topics without signaling that you are going to change topics, it could confuse others and make it difficult for them to follow along.

I will give some kind of signal before changing topics.

❻ Use a smooth transition – Try to link the current topic to the topic you want to talk about.

I will transition to a new topic by linking it to the current topic.

❼ Ask to switch topics if the conversation is hurtful or personal – If the conversation could be hurtful to someone else or is too personal, ask to switch topics.

If someone starts a conversation that is personal or could hurt someone else, I will say, "I'm not comfortable talking about this. Can we talk about something else?"

Switching Topics

Look and Learn

Teacher says: The students in this scene are changing the topic of their conversations.

Directions: 1. **Draw a circle** around each student who **is switching topics** appropriately.

2. **Draw an X** on each student who **is not switching topics** appropriately.

Simply Social 7™

Switching Topics

Think and Review

Directions: Read the stories, and then answer the questions below about the **Simply Social 7** for **Switching Topics**.

1. **In the classroom...** Charles and his classmates were talking about their pets while working on a class project. When one of his classmates asked if anyone else had a pet bird, Charles said, "My family is going on vacation next week!"

   Did Charles do the right thing?   a) Yes – What could he do next?

   b) No – What should he have done?

2. **At school...** Before school started Sydney's friends were talking and making fun of another student in her class. Sydney was uncomfortable with the conversation and wanted to switch topics, but she didn't say anything.

   Did Sydney do the right thing?   a) Yes – What could she do next?

   b) No – What should she have done?

3. **At home...** Luis's mom and sister were talking in the kitchen. Luis was standing nearby, but he wasn't paying attention to the conversation. When his mom asked him a question, Luis told his mom and sister that he passed his history test.

   Did Luis do the right thing?   a) Yes – What could he do next?

   b) No – What should he have done?

4. **In the community...** While at the fair Kaitlin's friends were talking about the rides they wanted to go on. After talking about the rides for a little while, there was a break in the conversation. Kaitlin wanted to switch topics so she said, "I think the roller coaster is scary, but it's not as scary as that new movie that just came out!"

   Did Kaitlin do the right thing?   a) Yes – What could she do next?

   b) No – What should she have done?

Discussion Questions

1. What are some situations in which you had to switch topics?

2. What would happen if no one ever used transitions when switching topics?

#BK-371 Simply Social 7™ at School • ©2011 Super Duper® Publications • www.superduperinc.com • 1-800-277-8737   59

Simply Social 7 — Switching Topics

Take-Home Practice

Dear Parent/Helper,

Today we talked about seven steps to follow when switching topics called the **Simply Social 7**. Please review these with your child. Have him/her read or repeat the statement in italics that follows each step. Then sign, date, and return this page. We will add this page to your child's *Simply Social Skills Book!*

Here are the **Simply Social 7** for **Switching Topics**...

1 **Pay attention** – *I will pay attention to what others are saying, so I will recognize when it is okay to switch topics.*

2 **Don't change topics if others are still interested in the current topic** – *I will stay on the topic of conversation if others are still interested in it.*

3 **Recognize the signals** – *I will watch for non-verbal signals to know when to introduce a new topic.*

4 **Wait for a pause in the conversation** – *I will wait for a break in the conversation to switch topics.*

5 **Don't change topics without warning** – *I will give some kind of signal before changing topics.*

6 **Use a smooth transition** – *I will transition to a new topic by linking it to the current topic.*

7 **Ask to switch topics if the conversation is hurtful or personal** – *If someone starts a conversation that is personal or could hurt someone else, I will say, "I'm not comfortable talking about this. Can we talk about something else?"*

_____   _____   _____
Parent/Helper Signature   Student Signature   Date

- -

Congratulations!

You are a Simply Social Superstar!

Student Directions: After you return the top of this page to your teacher, cut out the award to the right. Add it to the award page in your *Simply Social Skills Book* or to your award wall in your classroom or at home.

 # Interrupting

Simply Social 7 Steps

Teacher says: It is usually considered impolite to interrupt others while they are speaking; however, there may be times when you need to interrupt to make a comment or ask a question. For example, if someone is speaking too fast and you need him/her to slow down, you may need to interrupt. When interruptions are necessary, it is important to be courteous.

Directions: Teacher will read the **Simply Social 7** steps. Student(s) will read or repeat the statements in italics that follow.

1. **Know when an interruption is necessary** – If your comment or question can wait for another time, don't interrupt the speaker.

    I will decide if my comment or question can wait or if I need to interrupt.

2. **Make eye contact with the person you want to speak to** – If you make eye contact with the other person, he/she may recognize that you have something to say and may invite you to speak.

    I will make eye contact with the person I want to talk to before I interrupt.

3. **Wait for a break in the conversation** – Try to wait until the speaker pauses to take a breath or to allow other people to speak.

    I will wait for a pause in the conversation before speaking if it is not an emergency.

4. **Gently clear your throat or say, "Excuse me"** – If you have made eye contact or have waited for a break and still have not had an opportunity to speak, you can clear your throat softly or gently say, "Excuse me."

    I will softly clear my throat or quietly say, "Excuse me"
    if I have not had the opportunity to speak.

5. **Wait to be recognized** – If you said, "Excuse me," wait to talk until the speaker lets you know it is your turn.

    I will wait to be acknowledged before continuing with my comment or question.

6. **Apologize for interrupting** – When you are given the opportunity to talk, start your comment or question with a brief apology for interrupting.

    After I am acknowledged I will start by saying, "I am sorry for interrupting, but…"

7. **Keep your comments short and to the point** – Remember that you have interrupted another conversation, so when you are given the chance to share don't ramble on or go off topic.

    I will be brief, and I will stick to the topic when I share my comments.

Interrupting

Look and Learn

Teacher says: Some of the people in this scene are interrupting others.

Directions: 1. **Draw a circle** around each person who **is interrupting** appropriately.

2. **Draw an X** on each person who **is not interrupting** appropriately.

Interrupting

Think and Review

Directions: Read the stories, and then answer the questions below about the **Simply Social 7** for **Interrupting**.

1. **In the classroom…** While Makayla's teacher was talking to the class about the acting parts available in their class play, Makayla shouted out, "I want to be the astronaut!"

    Did Makayla do the right thing? a) Yes – What could she do next?

    b) No – What should she have done?

2. **At school…** Isaiah was new to the school and couldn't find the restroom. He approached a couple of boys who were talking and waited for a break in the conversation. One of the boys noticed him standing nearby and asked Isaiah if he needed help.

    Did Isaiah do the right thing? a) Yes – What could he do next?

    b) No – What should he have done?

3. **At home…** Landon's mom was on the phone when he got home from school. Landon wanted to know what he could have for a snack, so he tugged on his mom's shirt and said, "Excuse me." When his mom continued with her phone conversation, Landon kept tugging on her shirt and repeating, "Excuse me."

    Did Landon do the right thing? a) Yes – What could he do next?

    b) No – What should he have done?

4. **In the community…** Aubrey was trying on shoes at the shoe store and needed a bigger size. She approached the salesman who was talking to another customer and said, "Hey! Do you have these in a larger size?"

    Did Aubrey do the right thing? a) Yes – What could she do next?

    b) No – What should she have done?

Discussion Questions

1. What are some situations in which you had to interrupt others?

2. What would happen if someone interrupted you every time you started to speak?

Simply Social 7 — Interrupting

Take-Home Practice

Dear Parent/Helper,

Today we talked about seven steps to follow when interrupting called the **Simply Social 7**. Please review these with your child. Have him/her read or repeat the statement in italics that follows each step. Then sign, date, and return this page. We will add this page to your child's *Simply Social Skills Book!*

Here are the **Simply Social 7** for **Interrupting**...

① **Know when an interruption is necessary** – *I will decide if my comment or question can wait or if I need to interrupt.*

② **Make eye contact with the person you want to speak to** – *I will make eye contact with the person I want to talk to before I interrupt.*

③ **Wait for a break in the conversation** – *I will wait for a pause in the conversation before speaking if it is not an emergency.*

④ **Gently clear your throat or say, "Excuse me"** – *I will softly clear my throat or quietly say, "Excuse me" if I have not had the opportunity to speak.*

⑤ **Wait to be recognized** – *I will wait to be acknowledged before continuing with my comment or question.*

⑥ **Apologize for interrupting** – *After I am acknowledged I will start by saying, "I am sorry for interrupting, but…"*

⑦ **Keep your comments short and to the point** – *I will be brief and I will stick to the topic when I share my comments.*

_____ _____ _____
Parent/Helper Signature   Student Signature   Date

- -

Congratulations!

You are a Simply Social Superstar!

Student Directions: After you return the top of this page to your teacher, cut out the award to the right. Add it to the award page in your *Simply Social Skills Book* or to your award wall in your classroom or at home.

Simply Social 7
Using Gestures

Simply Social 7 Steps

Teacher says: *Gesturing* is when you move your hand or another part of your body to illustrate a point. Whether you use your hand to wave hello or to demonstrate how big the fish was that you caught on your fishing trip, you are using gestures. Gestures give other people a visual picture of what you are saying and can help you communicate more effectively.

Directions: Teacher will read the **Simply Social 7** steps. Student(s) will read or repeat the statements in italics that follow.

1 **Observe how people around you use gestures** – Think about the message that other people are communicating with their gestures, and whether the gestures are helpful or distracting.

I will pay attention to the gestures people use to communicate.

2 **Learn common gestures** – It is important to know how to interpret and use gestures that express everyday ideas such as "hello," "okay," "come here," and "great job!"

*I will learn basic gestures that communicate thoughts like "hello,"
"okay," "come here," and "great job!"*

3 **Think about what you are trying to say** – Know what you are trying to communicate and which gestures can help you get your point across.

I will think about what I want to communicate before choosing which gestures to use.

4 **Use gestures that help illustrate your point** – Gestures can add information to ideas that you are trying to share.

I will use gestures that help my listener "get the picture."

5 **Use gestures that match what you are saying** – Your gestures should always match what you say. For example, if you are talking about something sad, you should not wave your hands around in excitement.

I will make sure that my gestures match the words I am saying.

6 **Don't overuse gestures** – Using too many gestures can be very distracting.

*I will limit my use of gestures and only use them when they
are necessary to help me communicate an idea.*

7 **Be natural** – Relax and use gestures that come naturally to you. Forcing yourself to use gestures that you are not comfortable with can make you look artificial and insincere.

I will only use gestures that feel natural to me.

#BK-371 Simply Social 7™ at School • ©2011 Super Duper® Publications • www.superduperinc.com • 1-800-277-8737

Using Gestures

Look and Learn

Teacher says: Some people in this scene are using gestures.

Directions: 1. **Draw a circle** around each person who **is using gestures** appropriately.

2. **Draw an X** on each person who **is not using gestures** appropriately.

Simply Social 7™

Using Gestures

Think and Review

Directions: Read the stories, and then answer the questions below about the **Simply Social 7** for **Using Gestures**.

1. **In the classroom...** Alyssa's friend was nervous about giving a speech in front of the class. After her friend finished her speech, Alyssa gave her a thumbs-up to let her know she did a great job.

   Did Alyssa do the right thing?   a) Yes – What could she do next?

       b) No – What should she have done?

2. **At school...** Taylor was disappointed that her school's soccer team lost its game. When a friend asked her what she thought about the game, Taylor used big, exciting gestures while telling her friend about her disappointment.

   Did Taylor do the right thing?   a) Yes – What could she do next?

       b) No – What should she have done?

3. **At home...** Joshua was telling his sister about football practice that afternoon. His sister was distracted and had a hard time following the conversation because Joshua used a hand gesture for every word he said.

   Did Joshua do the right thing?   a) Yes – What could he do next?

       b) No – What should he have done?

4. **In the community...** While out walking his dog in the neighborhood, Daniel met up with a friend. Daniel told his friend about a fishing trip he went on and used a gesture to show him how big the fish was that he caught.

   Did Daniel do the right thing?   a) Yes – What could he do next?

       b) No – What should he have done?

Discussion Questions

1. What are some situations in which you used gestures to communicate an idea?

2. What would happen if you were talking to someone who used a gesture for every word he/she said?

#BK-371 Simply Social 7™ at School • ©2011 Super Duper® Publications • www.superduperinc.com • 1-800-277-8737

Simply Social 7 — Using Gestures

Take-Home Practice

Dear Parent/Helper,

Today we talked about seven steps to follow when using gestures called the **Simply Social 7**. Please review these with your child. Have him/her read or repeat the statement in italics that follows each step. Then sign, date, and return this page. We will add this page to your child's *Simply Social Skills Book!*

Here are the **Simply Social 7** for **Using Gestures**...

❶ Observe how people around you use gestures – *I will pay attention to the gestures people use to communicate.*

❷ Learn common gestures – *I will learn basic gestures that communicate thoughts like "hello," "okay," "come here," and "great job!"*

❸ Think about what you are trying to say – *I will think about what I want to communicate before choosing which gestures to use.*

❹ Use gestures that help illustrate your point – *I will use gestures that help my listener "get the picture."*

❺ Use gestures that match what you are saying – *I will make sure that my gestures match the words I am saying.*

❻ Don't overuse gestures – *I will limit my use of gestures and only use them when they are necessary to help me communicate an idea.*

❼ Be natural – *I will only use gestures that feel natural to me.*

_____   _____   _____
Parent/Helper Signature   Student Signature   Date

- -

Congratulations!

You are a Simply Social Superstar!

Student Directions: After you return the top of this page to your teacher, cut out the award to the right. Add it to the award page in your *Simply Social Skills Book* or to your award wall in your classroom or at home.

Simply Social 7 — Interpreting Body Language

Simply Social 7 Steps

Teacher says: *Body language* can help you communicate ideas and feelings without using words. The gestures you use, the way you stand, and the expression on your face can help others understand what you are thinking even when you don't tell them. For example, when you nod your head, smile, and make eye contact with someone while he/she is speaking, the other person can tell by your body language that you are listening.

Directions: Teacher will read the **Simply Social 7** steps. Student(s) will read or repeat the statements in italics that follow.

1. **Observe the people around you** – Match the gestures, posture, and facial expressions of people near you with the words they say to learn what their body language means.

   I will watch the people around me to learn more about body language.

2. **Look at the other person's eyes** – If the other person is constantly looking around, he/she may be bored or distracted. A person who looks down a lot may be nervous or shy. Someone who makes appropriate eye contact is usually listening and interested in the conversation.

   I will pay attention to where the other person is looking
   to help me understand how he/she feels.

3. **Think about the other person's facial expressions** – Smiles, frowns, or raised eyebrows can let you know if someone is happy, sad, angry, surprised, or excited.

   I will use the other person's facial expressions to help me
   recognize when he/she is happy, sad, or angry.

4. **How close is the other person standing to you?** – People usually stand closer to others when they are comfortable with them or when they are interested in what they are saying.

   I will remember that the distance between myself and my
   conversational partner can tell me how comfortable he/she is.

5. **Watch for movement in the other person's feet** – If the person you are speaking to is constantly moving his/her feet, it could mean that the individual is impatient, nervous, scared, or excited.

   I will remember that the person I am speaking to may be impatient,
   nervous, scared, or excited if he/she is constantly moving his/her feet.

6. **Be aware of the other person's hand movements** – Many people play with their hands when they are bored or nervous.

   I will remember that the person I am speaking to may be nervous
   or bored if he/she is playing with his/her hands.

7. **Pay attention to any changes in the other person's body language** – Changes in body language can help you know when to change topics or end a conversation.

   I will notice changes in others' body language
   and think about the messages they might be sending.

#BK-371 Simply Social 7™ at School • ©2011 Super Duper® Publications • www.superduperinc.com • 1-800-277-8737

Simply Social 7 — Interpreting Body Language

Look and Learn

Teacher says: The students in this scene are receiving body language signals from other band members.

Directions: 1. **Draw a circle** around each student who **is interpreting body language** appropriately.

2. **Draw an X** on each student who **is not interpreting body language** appropriately.

Simply Social 7 — Interpreting Body Language

Think and Review

Directions: Read the stories, and then answer the questions below about the **Simply Social 7** for **Interpreting Body Language**.

1. **In the classroom...** While talking about his science project, José noticed that his classmate kept looking around the room and checking his watch. José kept talking about how he came up with the idea for his project.

   Did José do the right thing?   a) Yes – What could he do next?

       b) No – What should he have done?

2. **At school...** While talking with a friend after lunch, Justin noticed his friend was holding his stomach and had a painful expression on his face. Justin asked his friend if he needed to go to the nurse.

   Did Justin do the right thing?   a) Yes – What could he do next?

       b) No – What should he have done?

3. **At home...** Gabriella asked her brother if he wanted to hear about the writing award she won. He had already heard about it, so he rolled his eyes and turned away. Gabriella noticed his body language and continued to tell her brother about the award.

   Did Gabriella do the right thing?   a) Yes – What could she do next?

       b) No – What should she have done?

4. **In the community...** Riley was showing her neighbor her pet snake. When the neighbor took a few frightened steps back, Riley took a few steps forward so her neighbor could get a better look at the snake.

   Did Riley do the right thing?   a) Yes – What could she do next?

       b) No – What should she have done?

Discussion Questions

1. What are some situations in which you were able to interpret someone else's body language?

2. What would happen if a person said he/she was interested in what you were saying but the person's body language showed he/she was not?

#BK-371 Simply Social 7™ at School • ©2011 Super Duper® Publications • www.superduperinc.com • 1-800-277-8737   71

Simply Social 7: Interpreting Body Language

Take-Home Practice

Dear Parent/Helper,

Today we talked about seven steps to follow when interpreting body language called the **Simply Social 7**. Please review these with your child. Have him/her read or repeat the statement in italics that follows each step. Then sign, date, and return this page. We will add this page to your child's *Simply Social Skills Book!*

Here are the **Simply Social 7** for **Interpreting Body Language**…

❶ **Observe the people around you** – *I will watch the people around me to learn more about body language.*

❷ **Look at the other person's eyes** – *I will pay attention to where the other person is looking to help me understand how he/she feels.*

❸ **Think about the other person's facial expressions** – *I will use the other person's facial expressions to help me recognize when he/she is happy, sad, or angry.*

❹ **How close is the other person standing to you?** – *I will remember that the distance between myself and my communication partner can tell me how comfortable he/she is.*

❺ **Watch for movement in the other person's feet** – *I will remember that the person I am speaking to may be impatient, nervous, scared, or excited if he/she is constantly moving his/her feet.*

❻ **Be aware of the other person's hand movements** – *I will remember that the person I am speaking to may be nervous or bored if he/she is playing with his/her hands.*

❼ **Pay attention to any changes in the other person's body language** – *I will notice changes in others' body language and think about the messages they might be sending.*

_____   _____   _____
Parent/Helper Signature   Student Signature   Date

- -

Congratulations!

You are a Simply Social Superstar!

Student Directions: After you return the top of this page to your teacher, cut out the award to the right. Add it to the award page in your *Simply Social Skills Book* or to your award wall in your classroom or at home.

Simply Social 7 — Ending a Conversation

Simply Social 7 Steps

Teacher says: Have you ever been in a conversation with someone who kept talking on and on and on? Or perhaps you have been in a conversation where there wasn't a lot to talk about, so you stood in awkward silence. Knowing how and when to end a conversation isn't always easy.

Directions: Teacher will read the **Simply Social 7** steps. Student(s) will read or repeat the statements in italics that follow.

1 **Watch for nonverbal signals** – Is the other person looking around the room? Has he/she stopped talking? Does it look like he/she is getting ready to leave? If the answer to any of these questions is "yes," then it may be time to end the conversation.

I will watch the other person's body language for clues as to whether or not the conversation should end.

2 **Be polite** – When you are ready to end a conversation make sure you remain polite.

I will not be rude or disrespectful when ending a conversation.

3 **Be honest** – You don't need to fake an illness or make up an excuse to end a conversation.

I will be honest with the person I am talking to.

4 **Wait for a break in the conversation** – If the other person is still talking, wait for a pause the conversation before speaking.

I will not interrupt another person while he/she is speaking unless it is an emergency.

5 **Apologize for ending the conversation** – If you need to end a conversation before the other person is ready, apologize for ending the conversation early.

I will tell the other person I am sorry for ending the conversation early.

6 **Tell the other person you must leave** – If you have somewhere you need to be, tell the other person you have to leave so he/she knows why you're ending the conversation early.

I will tell the person that I need to leave if I have a reason.

7 **End on a positive note** – Ending a conversation on a positive note can ease any hurt feelings, if the other person was not ready for it to end.

I will say something positive like, "See you later!" or "I'll talk to you tomorrow!" at the end of a conversation.

#BK-371 Simply Social 7™ at School • ©2011 Super Duper® Publications • www.superduperinc.com • 1-800-277-8737

Ending a Conversation

Look and Learn

Teacher says: The students in this scene are involved in conversations in the hallway.

Directions: 1. **Draw a circle** around each student who **is ending a conversation** appropriately.

2. **Draw an X** on each student who **is not ending a conversation** appropriately.

Simply Social 7 — Ending a Conversation

Think and Review

Directions: Read the stories, and then answer the questions below about the **Simply Social 7** for **Ending a Conversation**.

1. **In the classroom...** Madeline was talking to her friend before the morning bell rang. During a break in the conversation Madeline told her friend, "Well the bell's about to ring, so I'll talk to you later!"

   Did Madeline do the right thing?   a) Yes – What could she do next?

       b) No – What should she have done?

2. **At school...** In the lunchroom William's classmate kept talking about the math test they took before lunch. William told him, "Stop talking!" Then he got up and moved to another table.

   Did William do the right thing?   a) Yes – What could he do next?

       b) No – What should he have done?

3. **At home...** Anna's brother was telling her about a science experiment he did in school. Anna didn't really want to hear about the science experiment, so she walked away while her brother was talking.

   Did Anna do the right thing?   a) Yes – What could she do next?

       b) No – What should she have done?

4. **In the community...** Roberto went to see a movie with his friend. They were talking outside of the theater after the movie when Roberto's dad drove up in the car to pick him up. At the next break in the conversation Roberto said, "I'm sorry, I have to go — my dad is here to get me. I'll see you tomorrow!"

   Did Roberto do the right thing?   a) Yes – What could he do next?

       b) No – What should he have done?

Discussion Questions

1. What are some situations in which you had to end a conversation?

2. What would happen if you just walked away from someone when you were done talking to him/her?

Simply Social 7: Ending a Conversation

Take-Home Practice

Dear Parent/Helper,

Today we talked about seven steps to follow when ending a conversation called the **Simply Social 7**. Please review these with your child. Have him/her read or repeat the statement in italics that follows each step. Then sign, date, and return this page. We will add this page to your child's *Simply Social Skills Book!*

Here are the **Simply Social 7** for **Ending a Conversation**…

1. **Watch for nonverbal signals** – *I will watch the other person's body language for clues as to whether or not the conversation should end.*

2. **Be polite** – *I will not be rude or disrespectful when ending a conversation.*

3. **Be honest** – *I will be honest with the person I am talking to.*

4. **Wait for a break in the conversation** – *I will not interrupt another person while he/she is speaking unless it is an emergency.*

5. **Apologize for ending the conversation** – *I will tell the other person I am sorry for ending the conversation early.*

6. **Tell the other person you must leave** – *I will tell the person that I need to leave if I have a reason.*

7. **End on a positive note** – *I will say something positive like, "See you later!" or "I'll talk to you tomorrow!" at the end of a conversation.*

_____   _____   _____
Parent/Helper Signature   Student Signature   Date

- -

Congratulations!

You are a Simply Social Superstar!

Student Directions: After you return the top of this page to your teacher, cut out the award to the right. Add it to the award page in your *Simply Social Skills Book* or to your award wall in your classroom or at home.

Simply Social 7™ — Adjusting Your Language Level

Simply Social 7 Steps

Teacher says: A person's *language level* is the vocabulary and grammar he/she uses when talking to another person. When you are speaking to a close friend your language level will be different than when you are speaking to your teacher. For example, you might say, "What's up?" to greet a friend, but, "Good morning" would be a more appropriate greeting for your teacher.

Directions: Teacher will read the **Simply Social 7** steps. Student(s) will read or repeat the statements in italics that follow.

1 **Consider your location** – The language you use on the playground can be more casual and relaxed than the language you use in the classroom.

I will think about how my location affects my language level.

2 **Think about the person you are talking to** – Remember that the language you use changes with the person you are speaking to.

I will think about whom I am speaking to.

3 **Listen to your partner's language level** – When you are having a conversation with someone, listen to the way he/she talks and the words he/she uses.

*I will listen to my speaking partner's language level
and try to use the same level when I am speaking.*

4 **Keep in mind the other person's knowledge about your topic** – If you are speaking to someone about a topic he/she knows nothing about, explain the terminology you are using or use simpler words.

I will use simpler vocabulary words if my listener is unfamiliar with the topic.

5 **Look at your listener's body language** – Does your listener's body language indicate that he/she is comfortable with the language level you are using?

*I will look at my listener's eyes, posture, and gestures
to determine if I am using an appropriate language level.*

6 **Listen to your speaking partner** – Your listener may tell you that he/she doesn't understand something you said.

If my listener tells me that he/she does not understand, I will say it in a different way.

7 **Keep watching and listening** – As you continue your conversation, keep watching your listener for signals that you are using an appropriate language level.

I will continue to watch and listen for cues in case I need to adjust my language level.

#BK-371 Simply Social 7™ at School • ©2011 Super Duper® Publications • www.superduperinc.com • 1-800-277-8737

Simply Social 7: Adjusting Your Language Level

Look and Learn

Teacher says: The students in this scene are talking to others using different language levels.

Directions: 1. **Draw a circle** around each student who **is adjusting his/her language level** appropriately.

2. **Draw an X** on each student who **is not adjusting his/her language level** appropriately.

Simply Social 7™ — Adjusting Your Language Level

Think and Review

Directions: Read the stories, and then answer the questions below about the **Simply Social 7** for **Adjusting Your Language Level.**

1. **In the classroom...** Caleb's classmate asked him to explain a vocabulary word that the teacher used. Caleb used simpler words to help his classmate understand the meaning of the word.

   Did Caleb do the right thing?   a) Yes – What could he do next?

   b) No – What should he have done?

2. **At school...** Bella was talking to her friends at recess. Her friends didn't understand a word that she used, but when they asked her to explain Bella got angry, told her friends that they were not listening, and walked away.

   Did Bella do the right thing?   a) Yes – What could she do next?

   b) No – What should she have done?

3. **At home...** Marquis returned home from school and greeted his little brother by saying, "What's happening, kiddo?" He then went into the kitchen and greeted his mom by saying, "Hi, Mom! How was your day?"

   Did Marquis do the right thing?   a) Yes – What could he do next?

   b) No – What should he have done?

4. **In the community...** Charlotte was spending the night at her friend's house. When the girls decided they wanted some ice cream, Charlotte approached her friend's dad and said, "Hey, dude! Got any chocolate ice cream?"

   Did Charlotte do the right thing?   a) Yes – What could she do next?

   b) No – What should she have done?

Discussion Questions

1. What are some situations in which you had to adjust your language level?

2. What would happen if you used a casual language level with your teacher or principal?

#BK-371 Simply Social 7™ at School • ©2011 Super Duper® Publications • www.superduperinc.com • 1-800-277-8737   79

Simply Social 7: Adjusting Your Language Level

Take-Home Practice

Dear Parent/Helper,

Today we talked about seven steps to follow when adjusting your language level called the **Simply Social 7**. Please review these with your child. Have him/her read or repeat the statement in italics that follows each step. Then sign, date, and return this page. We will add this page to your child's *Simply Social Skills Book!*

Here are the **Simply Social 7** for **Adjusting Your Language Level**...

❶ **Consider your location** – *I will think about how my location affects my language level.*

❷ **Think about the person you are talking to** – *I will think about whom I am speaking to.*

❸ **Listen to your partner's language level** – *I will listen to my speaking partner's language level and try to use the same level when I am speaking.*

❹ **Keep in mind the other person's knowledge about your topic** – *I will use simpler vocabulary words if my listener is unfamiliar with the topic.*

❺ **Look at your listener's body language** – *I will look at my listener's eyes, posture, and gestures to determine if I am using an appropriate language level.*

❻ **Listen to your speaking partner** – *If my listener tells me that he/she does not understand, I will say it in a different way.*

❼ **Keep watching and listening** – *I will continue to watch and listen for cues in case I need to adjust my language level.*

_____   _____   _____
Parent/Helper Signature   Student Signature   Date

- -

Congratulations!

You are a Simply Social Superstar!

Student Directions: After you return the top of this page to your teacher, cut out the award to the right. Add it to the award page in your *Simply Social Skills Book* or to your award wall in your classroom or at home.

80 #BK-371 Simply Social 7™ at School • ©2011 Super Duper® Publications • www.superduperinc.com • 1-800-277-8737

Following Rules

Simply Social 7 Steps

Teacher says: There are rules to follow in the classroom, rules for walking in the hallway, rules in the cafeteria—rules everywhere we go! *Rules* help us understand what we should and shouldn't do in order to stay safe and show respect for other people.

Directions: Teacher will read the **Simply Social 7** steps. Student(s) will read or repeat the statements in italics that follow.

1. **Know that rules exist for a reason** – The rules in your school were not created just because making rules is fun. Rules were created to keep you safe and to make sure everyone is treated fairly.

    I will remember that rules exist to keep us safe and to encourage fairness.

2. **Know the rules** – Know what the rules are in each area of your school — in the classroom, hallways library, cafeteria, and other areas.

    I will make sure I know the rules for the different areas in my school.

3. **Understand the rules** – It's important to understand the rules so that you can obey them.

    I will understand what I am supposed to do.

4. **Ask questions** – You can't follow rules if you don't understand them. If there is a rule that you do not understand, ask someone to explain it to you.

    I will ask someone to explain a rule if I do not understand it.

5. **Don't follow poor examples** – If you see someone else breaking the rules, it does not mean it's okay.

    I will not follow the example of someone who breaks the rules.

6. **Make positive choices** – When faced with a decision to follow a rule or break it, making a positive choice will make you and your teachers happier in the end!

    I will think about the rules and my choices, and I will make a positive choice.

7. **Know that there are consequences** – When you decide that you are not going to follow the rules, there are often consequences that come with breaking the rules.

    I will be prepared to accept the consequences if I break a rule.

81

Following Rules

Look and Learn

Teacher says: The students in this scene should be following the rules of their school.

Directions: 1. **Draw a circle** around each student who **is following rules**.

2. **Draw an X** on each student who **is not following rules**.

Following Rules

Think and Review

Directions: Read the stories, and then answer the questions below about the **Simply Social 7** for **Following Rules**.

1. **In the classroom…** Joseph knows that he is not supposed to shout in the classroom. But his nose was running and his classmate was standing next to the box of tissues, so Joseph shouted, "Will you please bring me a tissue?"

    Did Joseph do the right thing?   a) Yes – What could he do next?

       b) No – What should he have done?

2. **At school…** Asia was in a hurry to get to class after orchestra practice. She knows she is supposed to put her music away in the music folder, but because she was in a hurry, she left it on her chair.

    Did Asia do the right thing?   a) Yes – What could she do next?

       b) No – What should she have done?

3. **At home…** Ellie knows she is supposed to finish her homework before she watches television. Her favorite program was coming on, and she didn't have her homework done. Ellie put her homework away and decided that she would finish it after the show.

    Did Ellie do the right thing?   a) Yes – What could she do next?

       b) No – What should she have done?

4. **In the community…** Gabriel knows that he is supposed to eat dinner before having any sweets. While playing at a friend's house before dinner, Gabriel heard the ice cream truck. Although he really wanted some ice cream, he decided that he would wait to get some later.

    Did Gabriel do the right thing?   a) Yes – What could he do next?

       b) No – What should he have done?

Discussion Questions

1. What are some situations in which you had to follow rules?

2. What would happen if there were no rules?

Simply Social 7 — Following Rules

Take-Home Practice

Dear Parent/Helper,

Today we talked about seven steps to follow when following rules called the **Simply Social 7**. Please review these with your child. Have him/her read or repeat the statement in italics that follows each step. Then sign, date, and return this page. We will add this page to your child's *Simply Social Skills Book!*

Here are the **Simply Social 7** for **Following Rules**...

❶ **Know that rules exist for a reason** – *I will remember that rules exist to keep us safe and to encourage fairness.*

❷ **Know the rules** – *I will make sure I know the rules for the different areas in my school.*

❸ **Understand the rules** – *I will understand what I am supposed to do.*

❹ **Ask questions** – *I will ask someone to explain a rule if I do not understand it.*

❺ **Don't follow poor examples** – *I will not follow the example of someone who breaks the rules.*

❻ **Make positive choices** – *I will think about the rules and my choices, and I will make a positive choice.*

❼ **Know that there are consequences** – *I will be prepared to accept the consequences if I break a rule.*

_____   _____   _____
Parent/Helper Signature   Student Signature   Date

- -

Congratulations!

You are a Simply Social Superstar!

Student Directions: After you return the top of this page to your teacher, cut out the award to the right. Add it to the award page in your *Simply Social Skills Book* or to your award wall in your classroom or at home.

Simply Social 7 — Paying Attention

Simply Social 7 Steps

Teacher says: Paying attention is an essential part of learning. *Paying attention* means you are listening and concentrating on what someone else is saying. In school, when your teacher is giving you directions, teaching you something new, or telling you a story, it is important to focus on what he/she is saying so you will be able to learn the information.

Directions: Teacher will read the **Simply Social 7** steps. Student(s) will read or repeat the statements in italics that follow.

❶ Get rid of distractions – Before your teacher begins to teach, clear off your desk and put away anything that can keep you from focusing on what your teacher is saying.

I will put anything that might distract me in my backpack or desk.

❷ Sit close to the front of the room – When you are closer to the person who is speaking you will find fewer distractions and will be able to pay better attention to what is being said.

I will try to sit as close to the front of the room as I can.

❸ Make eye contact with the speaker – It is usually easier to pay attention to what someone is saying when you are looking at him/her.

I will look at the person who is speaking to me.

❹ Watch your posture – When you sit with a relaxed or slouched posture, it is easier to lose focus.

I will sit up straight and keep my head up when I am trying to pay attention.

❺ Take notes – Taking notes will help you remember the information and remain focused.

I will take notes when I need to remember what someone is saying.

❻ Participate in the discussion when possible – If you answer questions and participate in discussions, it increases your motivation to listen and understand what someone is saying.

I will take advantage of any opportunity I have to answer or ask questions.

❼ Refocus when you lose focus – When you discover that you are no longer paying attention, stop and refocus your attention on the speaker.

I will make a conscious decision to regain my focus when I am no longer paying attention.

#BK-371 Simply Social 7™ at School • ©2011 Super Duper® Publications • www.superduperinc.com • 1-800-277-8737

Paying Attention

Look and Learn

Teacher says: The students in this scene should be paying attention to their teacher.

Directions: 1. **Draw a circle** around each student who **is paying attention**.

2. **Draw an X** on each student who **is not paying attention**.

Simply Social 7 — Paying Attention

Think and Review

Directions: Read the stories, and then answer the questions below about the **Simply Social 7** for **Paying Attention**.

1. **In the classroom…** When Hunter's teacher announced that it was time to start the science lesson, Hunter cleared off his desk and put his comic book in his backpack.

   Did Hunter do the right thing?   a) Yes – What could he do next?

   b) No – What should he have done?

2. **At school…** During theater practice Morgan's director gave directions to the cast about how to exit the stage. Morgan was concentrating on her lines while the director was speaking. When it came time to exit the stage, Morgan went the wrong way.

   Did Morgan do the right thing?   a) Yes – What could she do next?

   b) No – What should she have done?

3. **At home…** Brooke's mom gave her specific instructions about what to buy at the grocery store. Brooke listened carefully and wrote down the items her mom mentioned.

   Did Brooke do the right thing?   a) Yes – What could she do next?

   b) No – What should she have done?

4. **In the community…** During his piano lesson Austin's piano teacher reviewed the proper way to position his hands at the keyboard. Austin was thinking about where he wanted to eat after his lesson, and when he began to play, his teacher stopped him to correct his hand position.

   Did Austin do the right thing?   a) Yes – What could he do next?

   b) No – What should he have done?

Discussion Questions

1. What are some situations in which you had to pay attention?

2. What would happen if you didn't pay attention while your teacher gave you directions for an assignment?

#BK-371 Simply Social 7™ at School • ©2011 Super Duper® Publications • www.superduperinc.com • 1-800-277-8737   87

Simply Social 7 — Paying Attention

Take-Home Practice

Dear Parent/Helper,

Today we talked about seven steps to follow when paying attention called the **Simply Social 7**. Please review these with your child. Have him/her read or repeat the statement in italics that follows each step. Then sign, date, and return this page. We will add this page to your child's *Simply Social Skills Book!*

Here are the **Simply Social 7** for **Paying Attention**...

❶ **Get rid of distractions** – *I will put anything that might distract me in my backpack or desk.*

❷ **Sit close to the front of the room** – *I will try to sit as close to the front of the room as I can.*

❸ **Make eye contact with the speaker** – *I will look at the person who is speaking to me.*

❹ **Watch your posture** – *I will sit up straight and keep my head up when I am trying to pay attention.*

❺ **Take notes** – *I will take notes when I need to remember what someone is saying.*

❻ **Participate in the discussion when possible** – *I will take advantage of any opportunity I have to answer or ask questions.*

❼ **Refocus when you lose focus** – *I will make a conscious decision to regain my focus when I am no longer paying attention.*

_____   _____   _____
Parent/Helper Signature   Student Signature   Date

- -

Congratulations!

You are a Simply Social Superstar!

Student Directions: After you return the top of this page to your teacher, cut out the award to the right. Add it to the award page in your *Simply Social Skills Book* or to your award wall in your classroom or at home.

Simply Social 7 — Ignoring Distractions

Simply Social 7 Steps

Teacher says: Anything that takes your attention away from where it should be is a *distraction*. Distractions can come from other students talking to you when you should be listening to your teacher, a dropped pencil, a sneeze, or even a loud truck driving past the school. It is important to ignore distractions so you can focus and do your best.

Directions: Teacher will read the **Simply Social 7** steps. Student(s) will read or repeat the statements in italics that follow.

1 **Make sure you are not tired, hungry, or thirsty** – It is a lot harder to focus and pay attention when you are tired, hungry, or thirsty.

I will get a good night's sleep every night and eat a healthy breakfast every morning.

2 **Choose what you will focus on** – Decide what you will pay attention to and focus on that one thing.

I will decide what I am going to pay attention to, and then I will concentrate on it.

3 **Put away anything that might distract you** – If you have things near you that might keep you from paying attention, such as a pencil topper, a toy, or a note from a friend, put them away in your desk or backpack.

I will put away anything that is not related to what I am trying to focus on.

4 **Identify possible distractions and plan how you will handle them** – Make a plan ahead of time so you will know how to handle distractions when they occur.

*I will decide in advance how to handle potential distractions,
so I will not lose focus when they occur.*

5 **Distinguish between important and unimportant distractions** – Some distractions, such as a fire alarm, should not be ignored. Learn to recognize which distractions are important so you can ignore the ones that are unimportant.

I will recognize important distractions and ignore others.

6 **Don't respond to others who try to distract you** – If other people are trying to distract you when you should be paying attention, ignore them!

*I will not react to friends or classmates who talk to me or try to distract me
when I should be focusing on something else.*

7 **If distractions continue, talk to your teacher** – If distractions continue to keep you from paying attention, talk to your teacher about moving to another seat.

I will ask for a different seat if ignoring distractions becomes too difficult.

 **Ignoring Distractions**

Look and Learn

Teacher says: The students in this scene should be listening to the speaker during the assembly.

Directions: 1. **Draw a circle** around each student who **is ignoring distractions**.

2. **Draw an X** on each student who **is not ignoring distractions**.

Simply Social 7 — Ignoring Distractions

Think and Review

Directions: Read the stories, and then answer the questions below about the **Simply Social 7** for **Ignoring Distractions**.

1. **In the classroom…** During a lesson about plants Marina's classmate told her that she liked Marina's new shoes. Marina thanked her and told her classmate where she could go to buy a pair, what styles were available, and how much they cost.

   Did Marina do the right thing?   a) Yes – What could she do next?

       b) No – What should she have done?

2. **At school…** Jack brought a puzzle book with him to work on before the assembly started. As soon as the speaker stepped up to the microphone, Jack put his puzzle book under his seat.

   Did Jack do the right thing?   a) Yes – What could he do next?

       b) No – What should he have done?

3. **At home…** Savannah was working on her homework assignment when her brother came into the room and turned on the television. Savannah moved to the kitchen so she would not be distracted by the television.

   Did Savannah do the right thing?   a) Yes – What could she do next?

       b) No – What should she have done?

4. **In the community…** Before driving to school Kevin turned off the radio and his cell phone so he could pay attention to what he was doing. He was so focused on ignoring distractions that he did not notice when an ambulance came up behind him with its lights and sirens on.

   Did Kevin do the right thing?   a) Yes – What could he do next?

       b) No – What should he have done?

Discussion Questions

1. What are some situations in which it is important to ignore distractions?

2. What would happen if you did not ignore distractions during a test?

#BK-371 Simply Social 7™ at School • ©2011 Super Duper® Publications • www.superduperinc.com • 1-800-277-8737

Simply Social 7: Ignoring Distractions

Take-Home Practice

Dear Parent/Helper,

Today we talked about seven steps to follow when ignoring distractions called the **Simply Social 7**. Please review these with your child. Have him/her read or repeat the statement in italics that follows each step. Then sign, date, and return this page. We will add this page to your child's *Simply Social Skills Book!*

Here are the **Simply Social 7** for **Ignoring Distractions**...

1. **Make sure you are not tired, hungry, or thirsty** – *I will get a good night's sleep every night and eat a healthy breakfast every morning.*

2. **Choose what you will focus on** – *I will decide what I am going to pay attention to, and then I will concentrate on it.*

3. **Put away anything that might distract you** – *I will put away anything that is not related to what I am trying to focus on.*

4. **Identify possible distractions and plan how you will handle them** – *I will decide in advance how to handle potential distractions so I will not lose focus when they occur.*

5. **Distinguish between important and unimportant distractions** – *I will recognize important distractions and ignore others.*

6. **Don't respond to others who try to distract you** – *I will not react to friends or classmates who talk to me or try to distract me when I should be focusing on something else.*

7. **If distractions continue, talk to your teacher** – *I will ask for a different seat if ignoring distractions becomes too difficult.*

_____ _____ _____
Parent/Helper Signature   Student Signature   Date

- -

Congratulations!

You are a Simply Social Superstar!

Student Directions: After you return the top of this page to your teacher, cut out the award to the right. Add it to the award page in your *Simply Social Skills Book* or to your award wall in your classroom or at home.

Simply Social 7™ — Getting the Teacher's Attention

Simply Social 7 Steps

Teacher says: There are times during the school day when you need to get your teacher's attention — for example, when you are not feeling well, need to ask a question, or use the restroom. When you need to get your teacher's attention you must do it in an appropriate way.

Directions: Teacher will read the **Simply Social 7** steps. Student(s) will read or repeat the statements in italics that follow.

1 **Raise your hand** – The best way to get your teacher's attention is to silently raise your hand.

I will quietly raise my hand.

2 **Look at the teacher** – After you raise your hand, look at your teacher and wait for him/her to see you.

I will look at my teacher and wait for him/her to see me.

3 **Stay calm** – Unless there is an extreme emergency, for example, someone is seriously hurt or there is a fire, remain seated and still.

I will not bounce around in my seat or wave my hand wildly in the air.

4 **Wait to be recognized** – Wait until your teacher calls on you to make your request.

I will wait for my teacher to acknowledge me before making a comment or asking a question.

5 **Say, "Excuse me"** – Sometimes your teacher may not see that you are raising your hand. If you have been waiting a while, try gently saying your teacher's name or "Excuse me" to get your teacher's attention.

I will quietly say, "Excuse me," then wait to be recognized if my teacher has not seen me.

6 **Apologize for interrupting** – If you interrupt your teacher to get his/her attention, you should apologize for interrupting.

I will say, "I'm sorry for interrupting, but..." after getting my teacher's attention.

7 **Wait for a response** – After you make your comment or ask your question, wait patiently for your teacher's response.

I will give my teacher some time to respond after I make my request.

#BK-371 Simply Social 7™ at School • ©2011 Super Duper® Publications • www.superduperinc.com • 1-800-277-8737

Simply Social 7 — Getting the Teacher's Attention

Look and Learn

Teacher says: The students in this scene are trying to get their teacher's attention.

Directions: 1. **Draw a circle** around each student who **is getting the teacher's attention** appropriately.

2. **Draw an X** on each student who **is not getting the teacher's attention** appropriately.

Simply Social 7 — Getting the Teacher's Attention

Think and Review

Directions: Read the stories, and then answer the questions below about the **Simply Social 7** for **Getting the Teacher's Attention**.

1. **In the classroom…** Sienna needed to sharpen her pencil, so she raised her hand and waited for the teacher to call on her. When her teacher acknowledged her, Sienna asked, "May I please sharpen my pencil?"

   Did Sienna do the right thing? a) Yes – What could she do next?

                 b) No – What should she have done?

2. **At school…** Phillip needed to ask his golf teacher a question, but his teacher was speaking to another student. Phillip approached his teacher and said, "Excuse me." When the teacher didn't respond immediately Phillip tapped him on the shoulder and repeated, "Excuse me" several more times.

   Did Phillip do the right thing? a) Yes – What could he do next?

                 b) No – What should he have done?

3. **At home…** Mac's dad was watching television when Mac needed to ask him a question about his math homework. Mac went and stood between his dad and the television and began to ask his question.

   Did Mac do the right thing? a) Yes – What could he do next?

                b) No – What should he have done?

4. **In the community…** Natalie went on a tour at the local museum. When she had a question about one of the paintings, she raised her hand and waited for the tour guide to acknowledge her before asking her question.

   Did Natalie do the right thing? a) Yes – What could she do next?

                 b) No – What should she have done?

Discussion Questions

1. What are some situations in which you had to get the teacher's attention?

2. What would happen if you blurted out in the middle of class to get the teacher's attention?

#BK-371 Simply Social 7™ at School • ©2011 Super Duper® Publications • www.superduperinc.com • 1-800-277-8737

Simply Social 7: Getting the Teacher's Attention

Take-Home Practice

Dear Parent/Helper,

Today we talked about seven steps to follow when getting the teacher's attention called the **Simply Social 7**. Please review these with your child. Have him/her read or repeat the statement in italics that follows each step. Then sign, date, and return this page. We will add this page to your child's *Simply Social Skills Book!*

Here are the **Simply Social 7** for **Getting the Teacher's Attention**…

1. **Raise your hand** – *I will quietly raise my hand.*

2. **Look at the teacher** – *I will look at my teacher and wait for him/her to see me.*

3. **Stay calm** – *I will not bounce around in my seat or wave my hand wildly in the air.*

4. **Wait to be recognized** – *I wait for my teacher to acknowledge me before making a comment or asking a question.*

5. **Say, "Excuse me"** – *I will quietly say, "Excuse me," then wait to be recognized if my teacher has not seen me.*

6. **Apologize for interrupting** – *I will say, "I'm sorry for interrupting, but…" after getting my teacher's attention.*

7. **Wait for a response** – *I will give my teacher some time to respond after I make my request.*

_____   _____   _____
Parent/Helper Signature   Student Signature   Date

- -

Congratulations!

You are a Simply Social Superstar!

Student Directions: After you return the top of this page to your teacher, cut out the award to the right. Add it to the award page in your *Simply Social Skills Book* or to your award wall in your classroom or at home.

Simply Social 7 — Asking for Permission

Simply Social 7 Steps

Teacher says: When you ask for *permission* you are asking to be allowed to do something. Sometimes you might not want to ask for permission, because you might be afraid the other person will say no. In school it is important to ask for permission from your teacher when you want to do something, so that he/she knows where you are, what you are doing, and that you are safe at all times.

Directions: Teacher will read the **Simply Social 7** steps. Student(s) will read or repeat the statements in italics that follow.

1 **Ask at an appropriate time** – Unless it's an emergency, try not to interrupt your teacher to ask for permission to do something.

I will ask for permission when my teacher is not in the middle of another activity.

2 **Make eye contact with the other person** – We demonstrate good communication skills when we look at people while speaking to them.

I will look at the other person's eyes when asking for permission.

3 **Ask politely** – When asking for permission be respectful and polite.

I will use words like, "May I…" and "Please" to ask for permission.

4 **Ask a specific question** – The other person won't know whether or not to give you permission if he/she does not understand what you want.

I will make my request clear and specific so the other person knows exactly what I am asking permission for.

5 **Be ready to give a reason** – Sometimes your reason for wanting to do something will make a difference in whether or not you are allowed to do it.

I will make sure I know why I want to do something before asking permission.

6 **Wait for an answer** – It may take your teacher some time to decide if your request is a good idea.

I will be patient and wait for a response.

7 **Accept the decision** – When permission is given or denied you must stick with the answer you are given.

I will not get angry or upset if I do not get permission.

#BK-371 Simply Social 7™ at School • ©2011 Super Duper® Publications • www.superduperinc.com • 1-800-277-8737

Asking for Permission

Look and Learn

Teacher says: The students in this scene need permission for something.

Directions: 1. **Draw a circle** around each student who **is asking for permission** appropriately.

2. **Draw an X** on each student who **is not asking for permission** appropriately.

Simply Social 7 — Asking for Permission

Think and Review

Directions: Read the stories, and then answer the questions below about the **Simply Social 7** for **Asking for Permission**.

1. **In the classroom...** Sasha was tired of hearing her science teacher talk about the solar system. When her teacher started talking about which planets had rings, Sasha got up and left the classroom to get a drink of water.

   Did Sasha do the right thing?   a) Yes – What could she do next?

   b) No – What should she have done?

2. **At school...** Becca was working hard during cross-country practice and was running faster than everyone in her group. She wanted to keep improving, so during the break she asked her coach if she could run with a faster group in the next practice.

   Did Becca do the right thing?   a) Yes – What could she do next?

   b) No – What should she have done?

3. **At home...** Andrew wanted to go outside to play with his friend, but it was close to dinnertime. Andrew asked his mom if he could go outside to play for a little while.

   Did Andrew do the right thing?   a) Yes – What could he do next?

   b) No – What should he have done?

4. **In the community...** Oliver went to the fair with his dad. His dad stopped to talk to a friend and told Oliver to stay close by. Oliver wanted to go on more rides, so he left his dad and went to the other side of the fairgrounds to ride the roller coaster.

   Did Oliver do the right thing?   a) Yes – What could he do next?

   b) No – What should he have done?

Discussion Questions

1. What are some situations in which you had to ask for permission?

2. What would happen if you left the classroom without permission and there was a fire drill?

#BK-371 Simply Social 7™ at School • ©2011 Super Duper® Publications • www.superduperinc.com • 1-800-277-8737

Simply Social 7: Asking for Permission

Take-Home Practice

Dear Parent/Helper,

Today we talked about seven steps to follow when asking for permission called the **Simply Social 7**. Please review these with your child. Have him/her read or repeat the statement in italics that follows each step. Then sign, date, and return this page. We will add this page to your child's *Simply Social Skills Book!*

Here are the **Simply Social 7** for **Asking for Permission**…

❶ Ask at an appropriate time – *I will ask for permission when my teacher is not in the middle of another activity.*

❷ Make eye contact with the other person – *I will look at the other person's eyes when asking for permission.*

❸ Ask politely – *I will use words like, "May I…" and "Please" to ask for permission.*

❹ Ask a specific question – *I will make my request clear and specific so the other person knows exactly what I am asking permission for.*

❺ Be ready to give a reason – *I will make sure I know why I want to do something before asking permission.*

❻ Wait for an answer – *I will be patient and wait for a response.*

❼ Accept the decision – *I will not get angry or upset if I do not get permission.*

_____   _____   _____
Parent/Helper Signature   Student Signature   Date

- -

Congratulations!

You are a Simply Social Superstar!

Student Directions: After you return the top of this page to your teacher, cut out the award to the right. Add it to the award page in your *Simply Social Skills Book* or to your award wall in your classroom or at home.

100   #BK-371 Simply Social 7™ at School • ©2011 Super Duper® Publications • www.superduperinc.com • 1-800-277-8737

Simply Social 7 — Asking Questions

Simply Social 7 Steps

Teacher says: How do you find out the information you want to know? You ask questions! Sometimes you might find it's hard to ask questions at school because you think you're the only one who doesn't know the answer. That's usually not true. Besides, if you don't ask your question, you may never know the answer!

Directions: Teacher will read the **Simply Social 7** steps. Student(s) will read or repeat the statements in italics that follow.

1 Identify the kind of information you need – Questions often begin with *who, what, when, where, why,* or *how*. Use the question word that will help you find out the information you need.

I will think about what I am trying to find out and ask questions that will get me the information I need.

2 Wait to be acknowledged – Depending on the situation, quietly raise your hand or approach the teacher. Wait for your teacher to call on you before speaking.

I will wait to be recognized before asking a question.

3 Look at the person you're speaking to – Part of good communication is looking at the person you're talking to.

I will look at the person I am asking a question of.

4 Make your question specific – If the person you're talking to knows what you're asking about, he/she will be able to give you an appropriate answer.

I will be as specific as possible when asking my question.

5 Wait for an answer – The person you're speaking to may have an answer right away, or he/she may need some time to think about your question.

I will be patient and wait for the other person to give me an answer.

6 Listen to the answer – There's no point in asking a question if you are not going to listen to the answer.

I will listen to the answer I am given.

7 Decide if the response answers your question – If the answer does not give you the information you want, you might need to ask another question.

I will ask another question if the first answer does not make sense or does not answer my question.

#BK-371 Simply Social 7™ at School • ©2011 Super Duper® Publications • www.superduperinc.com • 1-800-277-8737   101

Asking Questions

Look and Learn

Teacher says: The students in this scene have questions to ask their teacher.

Directions: 1. **Draw a circle** around each student who **is asking questions** appropriately.

2. **Draw an X** on each student who **is not asking questions** appropriately.

Simply Social 7™

Asking Questions

Think and Review

Directions: Read the stories, and then answer the questions below about the **Simply Social 7** for **Asking Questions**.

1. **In the classroom...** After a history lesson about the Civil War, Sophia couldn't remember which side the Union soldiers fought on. Sophia asked her teacher, "What did you say about the soldiers?"

   Did Sophia do the right thing?   a) Yes – What could she do next?

   b) No – What should she have done?

2. **At school...** After the dismissal bell rang, Benjamin couldn't find his bus. He wanted to get home quickly, so he just got on the first bus.

   Did Benjamin do the right thing?   a) Yes – What could he do next?

   b) No – What should he have done?

3. **At home...** Sergio couldn't find his coat, so he asked his mom, "Have you seen my coat?" While his mom was looking for the coat in the closet, Sergio asked her again, "Have you seen my coat?"

   Did Sergio do the right thing?   a) Yes – What could he do next?

   b) No – What should he have done?

4. **In the community...** Cara once heard that if you are chased by an alligator, you should run in a zigzag pattern. She wanted to know if this was true, so when she went to the zoo she asked the zookeeper.

   Did Cara do the right thing?   a) Yes – What could she do next?

   b) No – What should she have done?

Discussion Questions

1. What are some situations in which you had to ask questions?

2. What would happen if you didn't understand the directions to a test and you didn't ask questions?

#BK-371 Simply Social 7™ at School • ©2011 Super Duper® Publications • www.superduperinc.com • 1-800-277-8737   103

Simply Social 7 — Asking Questions

Take-Home Practice

Dear Parent/Helper,

Today we talked about seven steps to follow when asking questions called the **Simply Social 7**. Please review these with your child. Have him/her read or repeat the statement in italics that follows each step. Then sign, date, and return this page. We will add this page to your child's *Simply Social Skills Book!*

Here are the **Simply Social 7** for **Asking Questions**...

1 **Identify the kind of information you need** – *I will think about what I am trying to find out and ask questions that will get me the information I need.*

2 **Wait to be acknowledged** – *I will wait to be recognized before asking a question.*

3 **Look at the person you're speaking to** – *I will look at the person I am asking a question of.*

4 **Make your question specific** – *I will be as specific as possible when asking my question.*

5 **Wait for an answer** – *I will be patient and wait for the other person to give me an answer.*

6 **Listen to the answer** – *I will listen to the answer I am given.*

7 **Decide if the response answers your question** – *I will ask another question if the first answer does not make sense or does not answer my question.*

_____   _____   _____
Parent/Helper Signature   Student Signature   Date

- -

Congratulations!

You are a Simply Social Superstar!

Student Directions: After you return the top of this page to your teacher, cut out the award to the right. Add it to the award page in your *Simply Social Skills Book* or to your award wall in your classroom or at home.

104 #BK-371 Simply Social 7™ at School • ©2011 Super Duper® Publications • www.superduperinc.com • 1-800-277-8737

Answering Questions

Simply Social 7 Steps

Teacher says: Sometimes your teacher wants to know if you are paying attention or if you understand the lesson he/she is teaching. One way for your teacher to find out if you understand something is to ask you questions about it. When you answer questions it shows the teacher that you are listening and whether or not you understand the material.

Directions: Teacher will read the **Simply Social 7** steps. Student(s) will read or repeat the statements in italics that follow.

❶ Pay attention – You can't answer questions if you're not paying attention to the lesson.

I will listen to the lesson so that I can answer questions if I am called on.

❷ Listen to the whole question – Don't guess the answer before the teacher finishes asking the question. If you guess wrong, your answer could be way off topic!

I will wait for my teacher to finish the question before I try to answer it.

❸ Ask for clarification – If you don't understand the question, it's okay to ask for clarification.

I will tell my teacher I do not understand, and I will ask him/her to repeat the question in another way.

❹ Recognize the clues to the answer – Questions often give clues that tell you what kind of answer you need to give. For example, if the question asks, "Why…" you will need to give a reason.

I will look for clues in the question that tell me what kind of answer I need to give.

❺ Raise your hand – Even if you really want to answer a question, don't just blurt out an answer. Make sure you raise your hand, and then wait to be called on.

I will always raise my hand to answer a question.

❻ Keep your answer short and to the point – When giving your answer don't ramble on or change topics.

I will give a response that answers the question without too many additional details.

❼ Be prepared to explain your answer – Your teacher might not understand your answer or might want you to expand on it.

I will be ready to explain my answer or give details from the lesson to support it.

Answering Questions

Look and Learn

Teacher says: The students in this scene have been asked a question by their teacher.

Directions: 1. **Draw a circle** around each student who **is answering questions** appropriately.

2. **Draw an X** on each student who **is not answering questions** appropriately.

106   #BK-371 Simply Social 7™ at School   •   ©2011 Super Duper® Publications   •   www.superduperinc.com   •   1-800-277-8737

Simply Social 7 — Answering Questions

Think and Review

Directions: Read the stories, and then answer the questions below about the **Simply Social 7** for **Answering Questions**.

1. **In the classroom...** Aiden's teacher asked the class a question that Aiden knew the answer to. The teacher called on another student to answer the question. Aiden really wanted to answer the question, so he blurted out the answer anyway.

   Did Aiden do the right thing?   a) Yes – What could he do next?

                                          b) No – What should he have done?

2. **At school...** Grace delivered a message to the front office for her teacher. The receptionist asked her a question that she didn't understand. Grace was too embarrassed to ask the receptionist what she meant, so she left the office without answering.

   Did Grace do the right thing?   a) Yes – What could she do next?

                                          b) No – What should she have done?

3. **At home...** Elizabeth's mom asked her why she left her books on the sofa. After listening to the question, Elizabeth told her mom that she left her books on the sofa so she would remember to take them in the morning.

   Did Elizabeth do the right thing?   a) Yes – What could she do next?

                                          b) No – What should she have done?

4. **In the community...** James and his friend were out riding bikes. When his friend started to ask him, "Do you like your..." James thought he knew what his friend would ask, so he interrupted him and said, "I love my new bike!"

   Did James do the right thing?   a) Yes – What could he do next?

                                          b) No – What should he have done?

Discussion Questions

1. What are some situations in which you had to answer questions?

2. What would happen if no one ever asked questions?

#BK-371 Simply Social 7™ at School • ©2011 Super Duper® Publications • www.superduperinc.com • 1-800-277-8737   107

Simply Social 7: Answering Questions

Take-Home Practice

Dear Parent/Helper,

Today we talked about seven steps to follow when answering questions called the **Simply Social 7**. Please review these with your child. Have him/her read or repeat the statement in italics that follows each step. Then sign, date, and return this page. We will add this page to your child's *Simply Social Skills Book!*

Here are the **Simply Social 7** for **Answering Questions**...

1 **Pay attention** – *I will listen to the lesson so that I can answer questions if I am called on.*

2 **Listen to the whole question** – *I will wait for my teacher to finish the question before I try to answer it.*

3 **Ask for clarification** – *I will tell my teacher I do not understand, and I will ask him/her to repeat the question in another way.*

4 **Recognize the clues to the answer** – *I will look for clues in the question that tell me what kind of answer I need to give.*

5 **Raise your hand** – *I will always raise my hand to answer a question.*

6 **Keep your answer short and to the point** – *I will give a response that answers the question without too many additional details.*

7 **Be prepared to explain your answer** – *I will be ready to explain my answer or give details from the lesson to support it.*

_____   _____   _____
Parent/Helper Signature   Student Signature   Date

- -

Congratulations!

You are a Simply Social Superstar!

Student Directions: After you return the top of this page to your teacher, cut out the award to the right. Add it to the award page in your *Simply Social Skills Book* or to your award wall in your classroom or at home.

Simply Social 7 | Following Directions

Simply Social 7 Steps

Teacher says: *Directions* tell you what you need to do in order to accomplish a goal. Directions might tell you how to take a test, how to behave, or how to get to a different location in the school. You must be able to follow directions if you want to do well in school.

Directions: Teacher will read the **Simply Social 7** steps. Student(s) will read or repeat the statements in italics that follow.

1 **Stop what you're doing** – Don't miss hearing the directions because you're distracted by something else. When you hear directions being given, stop what you're doing.

I will stop what I am doing so that I can listen to the directions.

2 **Listen to all of the directions** – You won't know what the directions are if you don't listen to everything that is said.

I will listen carefully to ALL of the directions.

3 **Identify what you are supposed to do** – Make sure you know what the directions are telling you to do.

I will think about the directions and make sure I understand them.

4 **Ask questions** – You can't follow directions if you don't understand them. If there is something in the directions that you do not understand, ask for clarification.

I will ask questions when I do not understand the directions.

5 **Remember the directions** – In order to be able to carry out the directions and complete the task, you must remember what to do.

I will repeat or write down the directions to help myself remember them.

6 **Know the consequences if you do not follow directions** – If you do not follow directions, you may get a poor grade, get in trouble, or get lost.

I will know the consequences of not following the directions.

7 **Do it** – Once you know and understand the directions, follow through and complete the task.

I will do the task once I know what I am supposed to do.

#BK-371 Simply Social 7™ at School • ©2011 Super Duper® Publications • www.superduperinc.com • 1-800-277-8737

Following Directions

Look and Learn

Teacher says: The students in this scene have been given directions for their science project.

Directions: 1. **Draw a circle** around each student who **is following directions**.

2. **Draw an X** on each student who **is not following directions**.

Simply Social 7 — Following Directions

Think and Review

Directions: Read the stories, and then answer the questions below about the **Simply Social 7** for **Following Directions**.

1. **In the classroom...** Gavin's teacher was giving him directions for delivering a note to another classroom. Gavin thought he knew where the other classroom was, so he didn't pay attention to the directions his teacher gave.

    Did Gavin do the right thing?   a) Yes – What could he do next?

    b) No – What should he have done?

2. **At school...** Jamie's teacher told his class they would have to be very quiet when walking through the third-grade hallway because the students were taking a test. While walking through the hallway, Jamie forgot about the test and started goofing off with his friend.

    Did Jamie do the right thing?   a) Yes – What could he do next?

    b) No – What should he have done?

3. **At home...** While Jennifer was reading a book her mom approached her and started to give her directions for babysitting her little brother. Jennifer set the book down so that she could listen to her mom.

    Did Jennifer do the right thing?   a) Yes – What could she do next?

    b) No – What should she have done?

4. **In the community...** Ruby finished her shopping and got in the express lane to pay. She noticed that the directions on the sign said she could only check out in the express lane if she had less than ten items. Ruby had 22 items, but she was in a hurry, so she stayed in the lane.

    Did Ruby do the right thing?   a) Yes – What could she do next?

    b) No – What should she have done?

Discussion Questions

1. What are some situations in which you had to follow directions?

2. What would happen if you didn't follow the directions on a test?

#BK-371 Simply Social 7™ at School • ©2011 Super Duper® Publications • www.superduperinc.com • 1-800-277-8737   111

Simply Social 7: Following Directions

Take-Home Practice

Dear Parent/Helper,

Today we talked about seven steps to follow when following directions called the **Simply Social 7**. Please review these with your child. Have him/her read or repeat the statement in italics that follows each step. Then sign, date, and return this page. We will add this page to your child's *Simply Social Skills Book!*

Here are the **Simply Social 7** for **Following Directions**…

1 **Stop what you're doing** – *I will stop what I am doing so that I can listen to the directions.*

2 **Listen to all of the directions** – *I will listen carefully to ALL of the directions.*

3 **Identify what you are supposed to do** – *I will think about the directions and make sure I understand them.*

4 **Ask questions** – *I will ask questions when I do not understand the directions.*

5 **Remember the directions** – *I will repeat or write down the directions to help myself remember them.*

6 **Know the consequences if you do not follow directions** – *I will know the consequences of not following the directions.*

7 **Do it** – *I will do the task once I know what I am supposed to do.*

_____   _____   _____
Parent/Helper Signature   Student Signature   Date

- -

Congratulations!

You are a Simply Social Superstar!

Student Directions: After you return the top of this page to your teacher, cut out the award to the right. Add it to the award page in your *Simply Social Skills Book* or to your award wall in your classroom or at home.

Simply Social 7 — Dealing with Transition

Simply Social 7 Steps

Teacher says: *Transition* is the process of moving from one classroom or activity to another. We go through many transitions during the school day. Sometimes it is difficult to deal with transitions, because you may not be ready to stop the task you're working on or you may not know what will happen next.

Directions: Teacher will read the **Simply Social 7** steps. Student(s) will read or repeat the statements in italics that follow.

1 **Check your schedule** – Schedules remind you which activities you'll be involved in throughout the day.

I will review my schedule so I know what is coming up.

2 **Plan ahead** – Think about what you need to do to finish the activity you're working on in order to get ready for the next activity.

I will think about what I need to do to be ready to transition to a new activity.

3 **Listen** – Often teachers give instructions that include information about what to expect during and after transitions.

I will listen when my teacher gives instructions about transitions.

4 **Take a deep breath** – Taking a deep breath can help calm any stress you might be feeling, and it gives you a moment to think.

I will take a deep breath in and let it out slowly if I am anxious.

5 **Stay positive** – Look at the good parts about the transition.

I will find something positive that will come from the transition and focus on it.

6 **Don't forget the rules** – When you're moving from one classroom or activity to another remember to follow the rules, such as using your inside voice, walking feet, and listening ears.

I will continue to follow the rules during transitions.

7 **Evaluate yourself** – After the transition take a quick moment to look at how you did and what you could have done better.

I will ask myself, "How did I do during the transition? What can I do better next time?"

#BK-371 Simply Social 7™ at School • ©2011 Super Duper® Publications • www.superduperinc.com • 1-800-277-8737

Dealing with Transition

Look and Learn

Teacher says: The students in this scene are transitioning from recess back to the classroom.

Directions: 1. **Draw a circle** around each student who **is dealing with transition** appropriately.

2. **Draw an X** on each student who **is not dealing with transition** appropriately.

Simply Social 7 — Dealing with Transition

Think and Review

Directions: Read the stories, and then answer the questions below about the **Simply Social 7** for **Dealing with Transition**.

1. **In the classroom...** Mia was close to finishing her essay when the teacher told her it was time to go to speech therapy. Mia put her notebook away and started to think about the fun things she would do in speech.

   Did Mia do the right thing?   a) Yes – What could she do next?

   b) No – What should she have done?

2. **At school...** Owen's teacher asked the class to line up to go back inside after playing softball at recess. Owen decided to run around the bases one more time before going in.

   Did Owen do the right thing?   a) Yes – What could he do next?

   b) No – What should he have done?

3. **At home...** Abigail's mom told her that she needed to brush her teeth and get ready for bed after her TV show ended. When the show ended, Abigail threw a tantrum because she wasn't allowed to watch the next show.

   Did Abigail do the right thing?   a) Yes – What could she do next?

   b) No – What should she have done?

4. **In the community...** Jacob knew he needed to leave the video arcade by 6:30 in order to get home before dark. Jacob set the alarm on his watch for 6:15. When the alarm went off, Jacob finished his game and got ready to leave.

   Did Jacob do the right thing?   a) Yes – What could he do next?

   b) No – What should he have done?

Discussion Questions

1. What are some situations in which you had to deal with transition?

2. What would happen if there were no transitions during the school day?

#BK-371 Simply Social 7™ at School • ©2011 Super Duper® Publications • www.superduperinc.com • 1-800-277-8737   115

Simply Social 7: Dealing with Transition

Take-Home Practice

Dear Parent/Helper,

Today we talked about seven steps to follow when dealing with transition called the **Simply Social 7**. Please review these with your child. Have him/her read or repeat the statement in italics that follows each step. Then sign, date, and return this page. We will add this page to your child's *Simply Social Skills Book!*

Here are the **Simply Social 7** for **Dealing with Transition**...

1 **Check your schedule** – *I will review my schedule so I know what is coming up.*

2 **Plan ahead** – *I will think about what I need to do to be ready to transition to a new activity.*

3 **Listen** – *I will listen when my teacher gives instructions about transitions.*

4 **Take a deep breath** – *I will take a deep breath in and let it out slowly if I am anxious.*

5 **Stay positive** – *I will find something positive that will come from the transition and focus on it.*

6 **Don't forget the rules** – *I will continue to follow the rules during transitions.*

7 **Evaluate yourself** – *I will ask myself, "How did I do during the transition? What can I do better next time?"*

_____   _____   _____
Parent/Helper Signature   Student Signature   Date

- -

Congratulations!

You are a Simply Social Superstar!

Student Directions: After you return the top of this page to your teacher, cut out the award to the right. Add it to the award page in your *Simply Social Skills Book* or to your award wall in your classroom or at home.

116   #BK-371 Simply Social 7™ at School   •   ©2011 Super Duper® Publications   •   www.superduperinc.com   •   1-800-277-8737

Simply Social 7 — Understanding Figurative Language

Simply Social 7 Steps

Teacher says: *Figurative language* describes one thing by comparing it to something else. If your teacher says you need to "hit the books," he/she does not really mean you should punch your books. Your teacher is using figurative language to say you need to study.

Directions: Teacher will read the **Simply Social 7** steps. Student(s) will read or repeat the statements in italics that follow.

① Determine if the other person said something that sounds silly – If the person you are talking to said something that sounds silly, he/she could be using figurative language.

I will consider when something sounds absurd it could be figurative language.

② Learn to recognize similes – Similes are one kind of figurative language. Similes use the words "like" or "as" to compare two things that are different. "She runs like the wind" is an example of a simile that tells us "She runs very fast."

*I will remember that when someone compares two objects
using the words "like" or "as" he/she is using a simile.*

③ Understand metaphors – Metaphors compare two things that are different, but do not use the words "like" or "as." For example, if someone wants to use a metaphor to express the idea that Tara walks slowly, he/she might say, "Tara is a turtle!"

*I will keep in mind that metaphors compare
two unrelated things without using "like" or "as."*

④ Know what idioms are – An *idiom* is a common phrase or sentence that means something other than what it literally says. For example, "Take it with a grain of salt" means "Don't believe everything you hear."

I will learn the meanings of common idioms.

⑤ Identify personification – When nonliving objects are given human qualities, it is called personification. For example, when someone says, "The leaves danced in the wind," he/she really means the leaves moved around a lot.

*I will remember that personification gives human
qualities to things that are not human.*

⑥ Look for another meaning – After you figure out that someone is using figurative language, look for the possible meaning of his/her words.

*I will try to figure out a person's meaning when
I know he/she is using figurative language.*

⑦ Get the picture – Remember that figurative language is often used to help listeners get a visual picture of what the other person is saying.

*I will create a picture in my mind that will help me understand
the meaning of figurative language.*

#BK-371 Simply Social 7™ at School • ©2011 Super Duper® Publications • www.superduperinc.com • 1-800-277-8737

Understanding Figurative Language

Look and Learn

Teacher says: The students in this scene are using figurative language.

Directions: 1. **Draw a circle** around each student who **is understanding figurative language**.

2. **Draw an X** on each student who **is not understanding figurative language**.

Simply Social 7 — Understanding Figurative Language

Think and Review

Directions: Read the stories, and then answer the questions below about the **Simply Social 7** for **Understanding Figurative Language**.

1. **In the classroom...** Jamal's friend told him that the science teacher's lesson was "as dry as a desert." Jamal laughed and agreed that the lesson was very boring.

   Did Jamal do the right thing?
   a) Yes – What could he do next?
   b) No – What should he have done?

2. **At school...** Isaac asked another student how close the football stadium was to the school. The student told Isaac it was "farther away than Mars." Isaac changed his mind about going to the stadium because he didn't have a rocket to get there.

   Did Isaac do the right thing?
   a) Yes – What could he do next?
   b) No – What should he have done?

3. **At home...** Kaylee asked her brother if she could play a video game with him. Her brother told her to "take a hike." Kaylee went to her room to find her hiking boots.

   Did Kaylee do the right thing?
   a) Yes – What could she do next?
   b) No – What should she have done?

4. **In the community...** On the way to the mall Allison's friend was impatient because cars were "crawling down the road." Allison told her friend, "Although we're moving very slowly, we'll still get there!"

   Did Allison do the right thing?
   a) Yes – What could she do next?
   b) No – What should she have done?

Discussion Questions

1. What are some situations in which you've heard or used figurative language?

2. What would happen if you didn't learn to recognize and understand figurative language?

#BK-371 Simply Social 7™ at School • ©2011 Super Duper® Publications • www.superduperinc.com • 1-800-277-8737

Simply Social 7: Understanding Figurative Language

Take-Home Practice

Dear Parent/Helper,

Today we talked about seven steps to follow when understanding figurative language called the **Simply Social 7**. Please review these with your child. Have him/her read or repeat the statement in italics that follows each step. Then sign, date, and return this page. We will add this page to your child's *Simply Social Skills Book!*

Here are the **Simply Social 7** for **Understanding Figurative Language**...

❶ Determine if the other person said something that sounds silly – *I will consider when something sounds absurd it could be figurative language.*

❷ Learn to recognize similes – *I will remember that when someone compares two objects using the words "like" or "as" he/she is using a simile.*

❸ Understand metaphors – *I will keep in mind that metaphors compare two unrelated things without using "like" or "as."*

❹ Know what idioms are – *I will learn the meanings of common idioms.*

❺ Identify personification – *I will remember that personification gives human qualities to things that are not human.*

❻ Look for another meaning – *I will try to figure out a person's meaning when I know he/she is using figurative language.*

❼ Get the picture – *I will create a picture in my mind that will help me understand the meaning of figurative language.*

_____ _____ _____
Parent/Helper Signature   Student Signature   Date

- -

Congratulations!

You are a Simply Social Superstar!

Student Directions: After you return the top of this page to your teacher, cut out the award to the right. Add it to the award page in your *Simply Social Skills Book* or to your award wall in your classroom or at home.

Making Friends

Simply Social 7 Steps

Teacher says: Friends make life more enjoyable and more satisfying in many ways. Friends are there for you when you need someone to talk to or hang out with. Friends know when you are excited, frustrated, or scared. Friends can lift your spirits when you're sad or celebrate with you when you're happy. Knowing how to make friends is the first step to having friends.

Directions: Teacher will read the **Simply Social 7** steps. Student(s) will read or repeat the statements in italics that follow.

1 **Act naturally** – You don't have to pretend to be something you're not when meeting new people. True friends will accept you for who you are.
  I will be genuine and be myself when meeting new people.

2 **Be pleasant** – No one wants to be friends with someone who is grumpy! Be positive, smile, and make eye contact when speaking to new people.
  I will be friendly, smile, and make eye contact when meeting people.

3 **Introduce yourself** – Tell potential new friends your name so they will know what to call you. If you don't know the names of the people you are talking to, ask them what their names are.
  I will say, "Hello! My name is ___. It is nice to meet you!" when I meet new people.

4 **Give a genuine compliment** – If you like something about the other person, such as his/her hairstyle, shoes, or jewelry, tell him/her. Your compliment should be real. If you make up a compliment, you will seem fake and insincere.
  I will tell a someone when I like something about him/her.

5 **Make small talk** – Talking about simple subjects such as the school, your classes, or music can help you to get to know the other person better.
  I will make light conversation with other people to learn more about them.

6 **Discover common interests** – While making small talk look for things you have in common. Shared interests give you something to talk about and allow you to build a stronger friendship.
  I will talk to other people about things we have in common.

7 **Make a plan** – Think of a way to continue your conversation with your new friend at another time. For example, invite your new friend to eat lunch with you. When you leave tell your new friend you will talk to him/her later.
  I will figure out the next step to take to build my friendship with my new friend.

Making Friends

Look and Learn

Teacher says: The students in this scene have the opportunity to make friends.

Directions: 1. **Draw a circle** around each student who **is making friends** appropriately.

2. **Draw an X** on each student who **is not making friends** appropriately.

Simply Social 7

Making Friends

Think and Review

Directions: Read the stories, and then answer the questions below about the **Simply Social 7** for **Making Friends**.

1. **In the classroom...** Cameron noticed that the new student in his class was wearing a Green Bay T-shirt. When they were lining up for lunch, Cameron approached the new student and said, "Hi! My name is Cameron. I really like your T-shirt! Are you a Green Bay fan?"

   Did Cameron do the right thing?   a) Yes – What could he do next?

   b) No – What should he have done?

2. **At school...** Audrey really wanted to be friends with another student at school. Audrey knew the girl really liked soccer, and even though Audrey didn't like soccer, she approached the girl at lunch and told her she liked soccer too.

   Did Audrey do the right thing?   a) Yes – What could she do next?

   b) No – What should she have done?

3. **At home...** Maurice's dad asked him to help with the yard work. Maurice really wanted to stay inside, so he was angry about helping outside. A new boy from down the street approached Maurice and introduced himself. When the boy asked him what his name was, Maurice mumbled his name to the boy.

   Did Maurice do the right thing?   a) Yes – What could he do next?

   b) No – What should he have done?

4. **In the community...** Katherine rode her bicycle down the street to meet the new girl who just moved in. After introducing herself Katherine started making small talk and found out they both enjoyed reading. When it was time to go Katherine told the new girl she would bring over her favorite book the next day.

   Did Katherine do the right thing?   a) Yes – What could she do next?

   b) No – What should she have done?

Discussion Questions

1. What are some situations in which you made friends?

2. What would happen if you were grumpy when trying to make friends?

#BK-371 Simply Social 7™ at School • ©2011 Super Duper® Publications • www.superduperinc.com • 1-800-277-8737   123

Simply Social 7 — Making Friends

Take-Home Practice

Dear Parent/Helper,

Today we talked about seven steps to follow when making friends called the **Simply Social 7**. Please review these with your child. Have him/her read or repeat the statement in italics that follows each step. Then sign, date, and return this page. We will add this page to your child's *Simply Social Skills Book!*

Here are the **Simply Social 7** for **Making Friends**...

❶ **Act naturally** – *I will be genuine and be myself when meeting new people.*

❷ **Be pleasant** – *I will be friendly, smile, and make eye contact when meeting new people.*

❸ **Introduce yourself** – *I will say, "Hello! My name is ___. It is nice to meet you!" when I meet new people.*

❹ **Give a genuine compliment** – *I will tell someone when I like something about him/her.*

❺ **Make small talk** – *I will make light conversation with other people to learn more about them.*

❻ **Discover common interests** – *I will talk to other people about things we have in common.*

❼ **Make a plan** – *I will figure out the next step to take to build my friendship with my new friend.*

_____   _____   _____
Parent/Helper Signature   Student Signature   Date

Congratulations!

You are a Simply Social Superstar!

Student Directions: After you return the top of this page to your teacher, cut out the award to the right. Add it to the award page in your *Simply Social Skills Book* or to your award wall in your classroom or at home.

Simply Social 7 — Maintaining Friendships

Simply Social 7 Steps

Teacher says: The best way to keep a friend is by being a friend. A good friend is considerate of his/her friends' thoughts and feelings. This does not mean that you have to agree about everything. Even friends can have disagreements, but they find ways to solve their problems and continue being friends.

Directions: Teacher will read the **Simply Social 7** steps. Student(s) will read or repeat the statements in italics that follow.

1 **Accept your friends for who they are** – The world would be a boring place if everyone liked and disliked the exact same things. Your friends may have habits or preferences that bother you, but that is what makes them unique. Don't try to change your friends into copies of yourself!

I will remember that our differences make us interesting,
and I will not try to change my friends' habits or preferences.

2 **Respect your friends' feelings** – We can't help how we feel about things. If a friend is bothered by something, even if you think it is silly, be kind and considerate of his/her feelings.

I will be considerate of my friends' feelings
whether I think the feelings are right or wrong.

3 **Spend time with your friends** – Getting together with your friends allows you to get to know them better.

I will spend time with my friends so I can learn more about them.

4 **Be honest** – Don't just tell your friends what you think they want to hear. Be honest with your friends, but be kind in your honesty.

I will be honest with my friends.

5 **Keep your promises** – Good friends are trustworthy and loyal. Don't make promises you don't intend to keep. If you make a promise, keep it!

I will follow through when I promise a friend that I will do something.

6 **Listen** – Sometimes we need to talk about the things that are bothering us. If your friend needs to get something off his/her chest, be a good listener.

I will be a good listener when my friends want to share
their thoughts and feelings with me.

7 **Admit when you're wrong and apologize** – We all make mistakes. If you have made a mistake or have hurt your friend in any way, admit it and tell your friend you are sorry.

I will tell my friend when I am wrong, and I will say I am sorry.

#BK-371 Simply Social 7™ at School • ©2011 Super Duper® Publications • www.superduperinc.com • 1-800-277-8737

Maintaining Friendships

Look and Learn

Teacher says: The students in this scene are talking to their friends at school.

Directions: 1. **Draw a circle** around each student who **is maintaining friendships** appropriately.

2. **Draw an X** on each student who **is not maintaining friendships** appropriately.

Simply Social 7

Maintaining Friendships

Think and Review

Directions: Read the stories, and then answer the questions below about the **Simply Social 7** for **Maintaining Friendships**.

1. **In the classroom...** Susan's friend was upset about her grade on the math quiz. Susan thought it was ridiculous that her friend was sad and told her, "You're so silly for being upset! It's just one grade — get over it!"

    Did Susan do the right thing?   a) Yes – What could she do next?

    b) No – What should she have done?

2. **At school...** During baseball practice Robert's friend asked if he would help him with his curveball over the weekend. Robert knew he already had plans with his family but promised to help anyway.

    Did Robert do the right thing?   a) Yes – What could he do next?

    b) No – What should he have done?

3. **At home...** Jasmine invited some friends over for a slumber party. During a pillow fight she noticed that one of her friends looked sad and wasn't participating in the pillow fight. She asked her friend if she wanted to talk about what was bothering her.

    Did Jasmine do the right thing?   a) Yes – What could she do next?

    b) No – What should she have done?

4. **In the community...** While at a friend's house, Tommy saw a soccer ball that he thought was his. He accused his friend of stealing his soccer ball and took the ball back. When Tommy went home he found his soccer ball under a bush. He decided to sneak the extra ball back to his friend's house without telling him.

    Did Tommy do the right thing?   a) Yes – What could he do next?

    b) No – What should he have done?

Discussion Questions

1. What are some situations in which you spent time with a friend in order to maintain the friendship?

2. What would happen if you never admitted you were wrong or apologized to your friends?

Simply Social 7: Maintaining Friendships

Take-Home Practice

Dear Parent/Helper,

Today we talked about seven steps to follow when maintaining friendships called the **Simply Social 7**. Please review these with your child. Have him/her read or repeat the statement in italics that follows each step. Then sign, date, and return this page. We will add this page to your child's *Simply Social Skills Book!*

Here are the **Simply Social 7** for **Maintaining Friendships**...

1. **Accept your friends for who they are** – *I will remember that our differences make us interesting, and I will not try to change my friends' habits or preferences.*

2. **Respect your friends' feelings** – *I will be considerate of my friends' feelings whether I think the feelings are right or wrong.*

3. **Spend time with your friends** – *I will spend time with my friends so I can learn more about them.*

4. **Be honest** – *I will be honest with my friends.*

5. **Keep your promises** – *I will follow through when I promise a friend that I will do something.*

6. **Listen** – *I will be a good listener when my friends want to share their thoughts and feelings with me.*

7. **Admit when you're wrong and apologize** – *I will tell my friend when I am wrong, and I will say I am sorry.*

_____   _____   _____
Parent/Helper Signature   Student Signature   Date

Congratulations!

You are a Simply Social Superstar!

Student Directions: After you return the top of this page to your teacher, cut out the award to the right. Add it to the award page in your *Simply Social Skills Book* or to your award wall in your classroom or at home.

128   #BK-371 Simply Social 7™ at School   ©2011 Super Duper® Publications   www.superduperinc.com   1-800-277-8737

Simply Social 7 — Taking Another's Perspective

Simply Social 7 Steps

Teacher says: People do not have the exact same thoughts and feelings about everything. They have different ideas and opinions based on their experiences in life. Taking another's *perspective* means trying to see things from his/her point of view. When we are willing and able to see things from another's perspective, we can learn things we didn't know before.

Directions: Teacher will read the **Simply Social 7** steps. Student(s) will read or repeat the statements in italics that follow.

1 **Remember, you don't know everything** – We can all learn something from the people around us if we take the time to look at things from their perspectives.

I can learn from other people when I try to see things from their perspectives.

2 **Keep in mind the other person's background** – People who grow up in different places and who are exposed to different experiences will have different perspectives on issues.

I will remember that our backgrounds and experiences affect our perspectives on issues.

3 **Put yourself in the other person's shoes** – Think about what you would do if you were the other person. How would you feel? What would you say?

I will think about what I would do, feel, or say if I were the other person.

4 **Don't forget the Golden Rule** – The Golden Rule tells us to treat others the way we want them to treat us.

I will try to see the other person's side because I want him/her to see my side.

5 **Listen** – When trying to see things from another's perspective it's helpful to listen to what he/she has to say.

I will listen to the other person so that I know what he/she thinks.

6 **Keep an open mind** – Don't make up your mind that the other person is wrong before you hear what he/she has to say.

I will wait to make a judgment until after the other person shares his/her ideas.

7 **Consider both sides** – When you are able to see things from different perspectives you know more about a situation and are able to make knowledgeable decisions.

I will consider both my perspective and other people's perspectives in order to make better decisions.

#BK-371 Simply Social 7™ at School • ©2011 Super Duper® Publications • www.superduperinc.com • 1-800-277-8737   129

Simply Social 7 — Taking Another's Perspective

Look and Learn

Teacher says: The students in this scene are talking with other students.

Directions: 1. **Draw a circle** around each student who **is taking another's perspective**.

2. **Draw an X** on each student who **is not taking another's perspective**.

Simply Social 7 — Taking Another's Perspective

Think and Review

Directions: Read the stories, and then answer the questions below about the **Simply Social 7** for **Taking Another's Perspective**.

1. **In the classroom...** For their class's community service project, Kylie wanted her class to collect donations for the local homeless shelter. When another classmate suggested the class pick up litter along the road, Kylie listened to her classmate's idea and kept an open mind about it.

   Did Kylie do the right thing?   a) Yes – What could she do next?

   b) No – What should she have done?

2. **At school...** During a student government meeting, Carter wanted his classmates to vote against the new cafeteria food plan. When a fellow classmate tried to share his reasons for supporting the plan, Carter interrupted and told him that no one needed to hear his side on the issue.

   Did Carter do the right thing?   a) Yes – What could he do next?

   b) No – What should he have done?

3. **At home...** Tina was mad because she wanted hamburgers for dinner and her family was having spaghetti. Her dad tried to tell her that they didn't have hamburger buns and they couldn't go to the store because the car was broken, but Tina wouldn't listen.

   Did Tina do the right thing?   a) Yes – What could she do next?

   b) No – What should she have done?

4. **In the community...** Darius saw a lost little girl standing on the sidewalk crying. Darius had promised his friend he would meet him at the mall in ten minutes, but when he thought about how the little girl must be feeling, he decided to stop and help her.

   Did Darius do the right thing?   a) Yes – What could he do next?

   b) No – What should he have done?

Discussion Questions

1. What are some situations in which you had to take another's perspective?

2. What would happen if we didn't try to see things from another's perspective when trying to solve a problem?

#BK-371 Simply Social 7™ at School • ©2011 Super Duper® Publications • www.superduperinc.com • 1-800-277-8737

Simply Social 7: Taking Another's Perspective

Take-Home Practice

Dear Parent/Helper,

Today we talked about seven steps to follow when taking another's perspective called the **Simply Social 7**. Please review these with your child. Have him/her read or repeat the statement in italics that follows each step. Then sign, date, and return this page. We will add this page to your child's *Simply Social Skills Book!*

Here are the **Simply Social 7** for **Taking Another's Perspective**...

1. **Remember, you don't know everything** – *I can learn from other people when I try to see things from their perspectives.*

2. **Keep in mind the other person's background** – *I will remember that our backgrounds and experiences affect our perspectives on issues.*

3. **Put yourself in the other person's shoes** – *I will think about what I would do, feel, or say if I were the other person.*

4. **Don't forget the Golden Rule** – *I will try to see the other person's side because I want him/her to see my side.*

5. **Listen** – *I will listen to the other person so that I know what he/she thinks.*

6. **Keep an open mind** – *I will wait to make a judgement until after the other person shares his/her ideas.*

7. **Consider both sides** – *I will consider both my perspective and other people's perspectives in order to make better decisions.*

_____ _____ _____
Parent/Helper Signature   Student Signature   Date

- -

Congratulations!

You are a Simply Social Superstar!

Student Directions: After you return the top of this page to your teacher, cut out the award to the right. Add it to the award page in your *Simply Social Skills Book* or to your award wall in your classroom or at home.

| Simply Social 7 | Giving Advice |

Simply Social 7 Steps

Teacher says: Sometimes we have difficult choices to make or we find ourselves in tough situations and don't know how to handle them. If a friend is in this position, he/she may ask you for advice. Your *advice* is your opinion about how your friend should deal with the situation.

Directions: Teacher will read the **Simply Social 7** steps. Student(s) will read or repeat the statements in italics that follow.

1 **Listen to the problem** – Listen for details such as: who is having the problem; what the problem is; when the problem happens; where the problem occurs; why it is a problem; how it became a problem.

   I will listen carefully to the problem so that I will be able to give appropriate advice.

2 **Determine if the other person is looking for advice** – Sometimes people don't want advice — they just want to talk about a problem to get it off their chests.

   I will listen to find out if my friend wants my advice or if he/she just needs to talk.

3 **Put yourself in the other person's shoes** – It may be easier to give advice when you try to think about the problem from the other person's point of view.

   I will think about what I would do if I were in the same situation.

4 **Take your time** – The person seeking your advice is looking for help. Don't just blurt out the first thought that comes into your head.

   I will take my time to give advice that is appropriate and helpful.

5 **Think about the consequences of your advice** – Before suggesting that your friend does something, make sure you think about the consequences of the action you are suggesting.

   I will think about whether my advice will help the situation or if it will make things worse.

6 **Stick to the point** – Focus on your friend's situation and a possible solution.

   I will not ramble, go off topic, or start talking about my own problems when giving advice.

7 **Know that the other person may not take your advice** – Your advice is just your opinion of what the other person should do. After you give your advice your friend will decide to do what is best for him/her.

   I will not get upset if my friend decides not to follow my advice.

#BK-371 Simply Social 7™ at School • ©2011 Super Duper® Publications • www.superduperinc.com • 1-800-277-8737

Giving Advice

Look and Learn

Teacher says: The students in this scene have been asked to give their advice.

Directions: 1. **Draw a circle** around each student who **is giving advice** appropriately.

2. **Draw an X** on each student who **is not giving advice** appropriately.

Simply Social 7

Giving Advice

Think and Review

Directions: Read the stories, and then answer the questions below about the **Simply Social 7** for **Giving Advice**.

1. **In the classroom...** John's classmate was disappointed with the *C* he got on his book report. He thought the teacher was being unfair. When he asked John for advice, John said that if he were in his classmate's shoes, he would discuss the grade with the teacher.

   Did John do the right thing?

   a) Yes – What could he do next?

   b) No – What should he have done?

2. **At school...** Leah's teammate asked her for advice about a necklace that disappeared during volleyball practice. She told Leah that she saw another teammate wearing a necklace that looked a lot like the one that was missing. Leah told her she should steal the necklace back during the next practice.

   Did Leah do the right thing?

   a) Yes – What could she do next?

   b) No – What should she have done?

3. **At home...** Tyrese's sister asked him for advice about what kind of present she should buy their dad for his birthday. Tyrese was busy and didn't want to talk to his sister at that moment, so he just told her to buy the first thing that popped into his head — a book.

   Did Tyrese do the right thing?

   a) Yes – What could he do next?

   b) No – What should he have done?

4. **In the community...** Hannah went shopping with her friend. Her friend found two pairs of shoes that she really liked and asked Hannah for advice about which shoes she should get. Hannah considered the price of each pair and thought about which pair would be worn most often then offered her advice.

   Did Hannah do the right thing?

   a) Yes – What could she do next?

   b) No – What should she have done?

Discussion Questions

1. What are some situations in which you were asked to give advice?

2. What would you do if a classmate asked you for advice about cheating on a test?

Simply Social 7: Giving Advice

Take-Home Practice

Dear Parent/Helper,

Today we talked about seven steps to follow when giving advice called the **Simply Social 7**. Please review these with your child. Have him/her read or repeat the statement in italics that follows each step. Then sign, date, and return this page. We will add this page to your child's *Simply Social Skills Book!*

Here are the **Simply Social 7** for **Giving Advice**...

1. **Listen to the problem** – *I will listen carefully to the problem so that I will be able to give appropriate advice.*

2. **Determine if the other person is looking for advice** – *I will listen to find out if my friend wants my advice or if he/she just needs to talk.*

3. **Put yourself in the other person's shoes** – *I will think about what I would do if I were in the same situation.*

4. **Take your time** – *I will take my time to give advice that is appropriate and helpful.*

5. **Think about the consequences of your advice** – *I will think about whether my advice will help the situation, or if it will make things worse.*

6. **Stick to the point** – *I will not ramble, go off topic, or start talking about my own problems when giving advice.*

7. **Know that the other person may not take your advice** – *I will not get upset if my friend decides not to follow my advice.*

_____   _____   _____
Parent/Helper Signature   Student Signature   Date

- -

Congratulations!
You are a Simply Social Superstar!

Student Directions: After you return the top of this page to your teacher, cut out the award to the right. Add it to the award page in your *Simply Social Skills Book* or to your award wall in your classroom or at home.

Simply Social 7

Turn-Taking

Simply Social 7 Steps

Teacher says: When working with others it is important to cooperate and take turns. *Taking turns is when a person does something and then allows another person to have a try.* Turn-taking allows everyone to participate in an activity. Turn-taking is a critical skill for activities such as playing games, working on group projects, and having conversations.

Directions: Teacher will read the **Simply Social 7** steps. Student(s) will read or repeat the statements in italics that follow.

1 When taking turns, everyone gets to play! – Taking turns gives everyone a chance to participate in a game or activity and makes everyone feel included.

> *I will remember that taking turns gives everyone*
> *an opportunity to take part in an activity.*

2 Share with others – If you have something someone else wants to use, you should share it with him/her.

> *I will share with others when they ask to use something I have.*

3 Ask first – If someone is using something that you would like to use, you must ask before taking it.

> *I will not take things away from other people. I will ask*
> *the other person to share or take turns with me.*

4 Use your manners – When asking to take turns be kind to the other person and remember to say, "Please" and "Thank you."

> *I will say, "Please" when asking to have a turn with an activity*
> *and "Thank you" when I am given a turn.*

5 Compromise – A compromise is when people work together to reach an agreement that is satisfying to everyone. Taking turns with an object is a good compromise if more than one person wants to use it.

> *I will compromise and take turns with others when we want to use the same object.*

6 Wait – If it's not your turn to use an object or participate in an activity, you must wait patiently until it is your turn.

> *I will wait patiently for my turn.*

7 Let the next person know it is his/her turn – When your turn is over let the next person know it is his/her turn.

> *I will tell the next person, "It's your turn!" when my turn is finished.*

#BK-371 Simply Social 7™ at School • ©2011 Super Duper® Publications • www.superduperinc.com • 1-800-277-8737   137

Turn-Taking

Look and Learn

Teacher says: The students in this scene should be taking turns with their classmates.

Directions: 1. **Draw a circle** around each student who **is turn-taking**.

2. **Draw an X** on each student who **is not turn-taking**.

Simply Social 7™

Turn-Taking

Think and Review

Directions: Read the stories, and then answer the questions below about the **Simply Social 7** for **Turn-Taking**.

1. **In the classroom...** Evelyn's classmates were all signing a card for their teacher's birthday. Evelyn wanted her turn to sign the card, so she pushed another classmate aside and said, "My turn!"

   Did Evelyn do the right thing?   a) Yes – What could she do next?

   b) No – What should she have done?

2. **At school...** Juan's art class was making their own modeling dough. Juan wanted a turn to stir the ingredients, so he took the spoon away from the student who was stirring.

   Did Juan do the right thing?   a) Yes – What could he do next?

   b) No – What should he have done?

3. **At home...** Chase's brother wanted to play with Chase's toy car. When his brother asked Chase if he could have a turn, Chase told him he would let him have a turn in two minutes.

   Did Chase do the right thing?   a) Yes – What could he do next?

   b) No – What should he have done?

4. **In the community...** Kimberly wanted to play with a pool float in the community pool. Another child was using the float, so Kimberly asked, "May I please use the float for a little while?"

   Did Kimberly do the right thing?   a) Yes – What could she do next?

   b) No – What should she have done?

Discussion Questions

1. What are some situations in which you had to take turns?

2. What would happen if someone took things from you without asking every time he/she wanted them?

#BK-371 Simply Social 7™ at School • ©2011 Super Duper® Publications • www.superduperinc.com • 1-800-277-8737   139

Simply Social 7: Turn-Taking

Take-Home Practice

Dear Parent/Helper,

Today we talked about seven steps to follow when turn-taking called the **Simply Social 7**. Please review these with your child. Have him/her read or repeat the statement in italics that follows each step. Then sign, date, and return this page. We will add this page to your child's *Simply Social Skills Book!*

Here are the **Simply Social 7** for **Turn-Taking**...

1. **When taking turns, everyone gets to play!** – *I will I will remember that taking turns gives everyone an opportunity to take part in an activity.*

2. **Share with others** – *I will share with others when they ask to use something I have.*

3. **Ask first** – *I will not take things away from other people. I will ask the other person to share or take turns with me.*

4. **Use your manners** – *I will say, "Please" when asking to have a turn and "Thank you" when I am given a turn.*

5. **Compromise** – *I will compromise and take turns with others when we want to use the same object.*

6. **Wait** – *I will wait patiently for my turn.*

7. **Let the next person know it is his/her turn** – *I will tell the next person, "It's your turn!" when my turn is finished.*

_____   _____   _____
Parent/Helper Signature   Student Signature   Date

- -

Congratulations!

You are a Simply Social Superstar!

Student Directions: After you return the top of this page to your teacher, cut out the award to the right. Add it to the award page in your *Simply Social Skills Book* or to your award wall in your classroom or at home.

140 #BK-371 Simply Social 7™ at School • ©2011 Super Duper® Publications • www.superduperinc.com • 1-800-277-8737

Simply Social 7 — Asking for Help

Simply Social 7 Steps

Teacher says: What would you do if the zipper on your backpack was stuck and you couldn't get your homework out? You could leave your homework in your backpack and get a bad grade, or you could ask someone for help. Sometimes we don't ask for help because we are afraid other people will think we are weak or not very smart. But asking for help actually shows that you are smart, because you can recognize when you are not able to accomplish a task on your own.

Directions: Teacher will read the **Simply Social 7** steps. Student(s) will read or repeat the statements in italics that follow.

1. **Think about the result** – What will happen if you don't ask for help? What will happen if you do?

   I will consider the consequences and decide if I should ask for help or not.

2. **Know that it's okay to ask for help** – You cannot do everything by yourself. It's good to recognize when you need help.

   I will remember that it is okay to ask for help.

3. **Don't wait until you are frustrated** – If you wait too long to fix the situation, you will become frustrated.

   I will ask for help before I become frustrated.

4. **Recognize what kind of help you need** – Decide if you need someone to do something for you, or if you need help understanding something.

   I will identify my problem and know the specific kind of help I need.

5. **Choose whom to ask** – Different people can help you in different ways. For example, you shouldn't ask a classmate to help you get a book off of a high shelf, but your classmate could help you put on your art smock.

   I will figure out who the right person is to help me solve the problem.

6. **Be specific** – Tell the other person exactly what you need help with. For example, if you need help opening a fruit cup, don't just hand him/her the fruit cup — ask, "Will you please help me open my fruit cup?"

   I will tell the other person clearly and specifically what I need help with.

7. **Don't forget to say, "Please" and "Thank you"** – It's important to always use good manners when asking for help.

   I will remember to say, "Please" when I ask for help and "Thank you" after I have been helped.

#BK-371 Simply Social 7™ at School • ©2011 Super Duper® Publications • www.superduperinc.com • 1-800-277-8737

Asking for Help

Look and Learn

Teacher says: The students in this scene need help in their gymnastics class.

Directions: 1. **Draw a circle** around each student who **is asking for help** appropriately.

2. **Draw an X** on each student who **is not asking for help** appropriately.

Asking for Help

Think and Review

Directions: Read the stories, and then answer the questions below about the **Simply Social 7** for **Asking for Help**.

1. **In the classroom...** Imani didn't understand her math assignment. Every time she re-read the directions she became more frustrated. When her teacher said it was time to turn in the assignment, Imani had only worked on two problems.

    Did Imani do the right thing?   a) Yes – What could she do next?

    b) No – What should she have done?

2. **At school...** Ryan was working on a clay project in art class. When he tried to sculpt a cat out of the clay, the clay crumbled. Ryan asked his art teacher what he could do to make the clay work better.

    Did Ryan do the right thing?   a) Yes – What could he do next?

    b) No – What should he have done?

3. **At home...** Holly was helping her mom set the table for dinner. She couldn't reach the shelves where the plates were kept, so she asked her mom to help her get the plates down.

    Did Holly do the right thing?   a) Yes – What could she do next?

    b) No – What should she have done?

4. **In the community...** Avery was flying his kite in the park when it got stuck in a tree. Avery became very upset. When an adult passing by asked if he was okay, Avery pointed to the tree.

    Did Avery do the right thing?   a) Yes – What could he do next?

    b) No – What should he have done?

Discussion Questions

1. What are some situations in which you had to ask for help?

2. What would happen if you didn't ask for help in an emergency situation?

Simply Social 7: Asking for Help

Take-Home Practice

Dear Parent/Helper,

Today we talked about seven steps to follow when asking for help called the **Simply Social 7**. Please review these with your child. Have him/her read or repeat the statement in italics that follows each step. Then sign, date, and return this page. We will add this page to your child's *Simply Social Skills Book!*

Here are the **Simply Social 7** for **Asking for Help**…

1 Think about the result – *I will consider the consequences and decide if I should ask for help or not.*

2 Know that it's okay to ask for help – *I will remember that it is okay to ask for help.*

3 Don't wait until you are frustrated – *I will ask for help before I become frustrated.*

4 Recognize what kind of help you need – *I will identify my problem and know the specific kind of help I need.*

5 Choose whom to ask – *I will figure out who the right person is to help me solve the problem.*

6 Be specific – *I will tell the other person clearly and specifically what I need help with.*

7 Don't forget to say, "Please" and "Thank you" – *I will remember to say, "Please" when I ask for help and "Thank you" after I have been helped.*

_____   _____   _____
Parent/Helper Signature   Student Signature   Date

- -

Congratulations!

You are a Simply Social Superstar!

Student Directions: After you return the top of this page to your teacher, cut out the award to the right. Add it to the award page in your *Simply Social Skills Book* or to your award wall in your classroom or at home.

Simply Social 7 — Helping Others

Simply Social 7 Steps

Teacher says: Everyone has times when they need help. Some things are just too challenging, too heavy, too time-consuming, too big, or too upsetting to handle on our own. Sometimes you may notice that someone is having difficulty with a task. Other times a person may tell you that he/she needs help.

Directions: Teacher will read the **Simply Social 7** steps. Student(s) will read or repeat the statements in italics that follow.

1 **Pay attention** – Be aware of what is going on around you so that you will notice when someone needs your help.

I will pay attention to the sights and sounds around me that may signal someone needs help.

2 **Think about the consequences** – Think about the positive and negative consequences of helping or not helping the other person.

I will ask myself, "What will happen if I help this person? What will happen if I do not help?"

3 **Put yourself in the other person's shoes** – Looking at the situation from the other person's perspective will help you understand why he/she needs help.

I will think about what I would want someone to do for me if I were in the same situation.

4 **Offer to help first** – It might look like someone needs assistance, but he/she may want to handle the situation without help.

I will ask the other person if he/she wants help, unless it is an urgent situation.

5 **Do the right thing** – If someone needs and wants help, then helping him/her is usually the right thing to do as long as no one gets hurt and you don't break any rules.

I will help the other person if it does not hurt anyone or break any rules.

6 **Listen** – If the other person is talking to you about a difficult situation, listen to what he/she is saying so that you will know how to help.

I will listen to the other person talk about the situation so that I will know how to help him/her.

7 **Be genuine** – Be yourself when helping someone else and don't say things you don't mean.

I will only say things that I mean.

#BK-371 Simply Social 7™ at School • ©2011 Super Duper® Publications • www.superduperinc.com • 1-800-277-8737

Helping Others

Look and Learn

Teacher says: The students in this scene have the opportunity to help other students.

Directions: 1. **Draw a circle** around each student who **is helping others**.

2. **Draw an X** on each student who **is not helping others**.

Simply Social 7™

Helping Others

Think and Review

Directions: Read the stories, and then answer the questions below about the **Simply Social 7** for **Helping Others**.

1. **In the classroom...** A classmate sitting next to Mason dropped a box full of pencils on the floor. Mason didn't offer to help pick them up because he figured someone else would offer to help.

   Did Mason do the right thing?   a) Yes – What could he do next?

   b) No – What should he have done?

2. **At school...** After the dismissal bell rang, Henry hurried down the hallway to go home. The girl in front of Henry tripped and books and papers went flying everywhere. Henry asked the girl if she would like some help collecting her belongings.

   Did Henry do the right thing?   a) Yes – What could he do next?

   b) No – What should he have done?

3. **At home...** Rachel's brother was trying to set a new personal record for how fast he could put the dishes away by himself. Without asking, Rachel grabbed a stack of dishes and started to help him put them away.

   Did Rachel do the right thing?   a) Yes – What could she do next?

   b) No – What should she have done?

4. **In the community...** Cecilia was walking her dog in the neighborhood when a little boy tripped over a toy and landed flat on his face. Cecilia was laughing so hard that she couldn't offer to help the little boy.

   Did Cecilia do the right thing?   a) Yes – What could she do next?

   b) No – What should she have done?

Discussion Questions

1. What are some situations in which you have helped others?

2. What would happen if your hands were full and you needed help opening a door but no one would help you?

#BK-371 Simply Social 7™ at School • ©2011 Super Duper® Publications • www.superduperinc.com • 1-800-277-8737   147

Simply Social 7 — Helping Others

Take-Home Practice

Dear Parent/Helper,

Today we talked about seven steps to follow when helping others called the **Simply Social 7**. Please review these with your child. Have him/her read or repeat the statement in italics that follows each step. Then sign, date, and return this page. We will add this page to your child's *Simply Social Skills Book!*

Here are the **Simply Social 7** for **Helping Others**...

1 **Pay attention** – *I will pay attention to the sights and sounds around me that may signal someone needs help.*

2 **Think about the consequences** – *I will ask myself, "What will happen if I help this person? What will happen if I do not help?"*

3 **Put yourself in the other person's shoes** – *I will think about what I would want someone to do for me if I were in the same situation.*

4 **Offer to help first** – *I will ask the other person if he/she wants help, unless it is an urgent situation.*

5 **Do the right thing** – *I will help the other person if it does not hurt anyone or break any rules.*

6 **Listen** – *I will listen to the other person talk about the situation so that I will know how to help him/her.*

7 **Be genuine** – *I will only say things that I mean.*

_____   _____   _____
Parent/Helper Signature   Student Signature   Date

- -

Congratulations!

You are a Simply Social Superstar!

Student Directions: After you return the top of this page to your teacher, cut out the award to the right. Add it to the award page in your *Simply Social Skills Book* or to your award wall in your classroom or at home.

Simply Social 7 — Working with Others in a Group

Simply Social 7 Steps

Teacher says: Wherever we are — at home, school, or at our jobs — we have to work with others in a group. A group consists of two or more people working together. We work with others when we play a sport, work on a science project, or help around the house. When you are able to work well with others in a group you are considered a "team player" and everyone wins!

Directions: Teacher will read the **Simply Social 7** steps. Student(s) will read or repeat the statements in italics that follow.

1 **Choose a leader** – When you work in a group it is a good idea to pick a leader before you start a task. The leader should be someone who knows all of the steps to finish the job, solves problems quickly, listens to his/her teammates, and respects everyone's feelings.

I will help to choose a leader of the group and consider that the leader may or may not be me.

2 **Identify who will do each task** – Everyone in the group should have a task and know what is expected to get the task done.

I will choose a task and make sure I understand what I am supposed to do.

3 **Follow instructions** – Make sure you know all the things you are supposed to do before you start your task.

I will follow all of the instructions to complete my task.

4 **Be patient** – Some people may take longer than others to get a task done. You may have to wait for someone else to finish his/her task.

I will not rush others to get their tasks done if I finish mine early.

5 **Help your teammates** – At times you may be able to finish your task and help others in your group finish their tasks.

I will offer to help my teammates finish their tasks if I finish mine first.

6 **Stay focused and don't give up** – When you work in a group everyone is counting on you. If you don't finish your task, then the group will not succeed.

I will keep working and let the group leader know if I need help.

7 **Let others know what you're thinking, but be polite** – It is important to share your opinions with the group. Be honest, but be kind.

I will share my opinions in a way that will not hurt other people's feelings.

#BK-371 Simply Social 7™ at School • ©2011 Super Duper® Publications • www.superduperinc.com • 1-800-277-8737

Working with Others in a Group

Look and Learn

Teacher says: The students in this scene are preparing for the school's Valentine's dance.

Directions: 1. **Draw a circle** around each student who **is working with others in a group**.

2. **Draw an X** on each student who **is not working with others in a group**.

Simply Social 7 — Working with Others in a Group

Think and Review

Directions: Read the stories, and then answer the questions below about the **Simply Social 7** for **Working with Others in a Group**.

1. **In the classroom...** Nicholas was working with his classmates on a science project. One of his classmates offered a suggestion for improving the project. Nicholas told him that his suggestion was silly.

   Did Nicholas do the right thing?   a) Yes – What could he do next?

   b) No – What should he have done?

2. **At school...** Alice was singing with a group of students during music class. One of her classmates didn't know where they were in the music. Alice helped by pointing to the place in the music.

   Did Alice do the right thing?   a) Yes – What could she do next?

   b) No – What should she have done?

3. **At home...** Elijah was working with his dad on building a go-cart. Elijah's dad told him to hold the steering wheel while he tightened the screw. Elijah held onto the steering wheel for his dad.

   Did Elijah do the right thing?   a) Yes – What could he do next?

   b) No – What should he have done?

4. **In the community...** Kate and her friends were earning money by helping a neighbor with his yard work. Kate didn't feel like working, so she hid behind a bush and took a nap while her friends did the work.

   Did Kate do the right thing?   a) Yes – What could she do next?

   b) No – What should she have done?

Discussion Questions

1. What are some situations in which you had to work with others in a group?

2. What would happen if you tried to do your task and everyone else's?

#BK-371 Simply Social 7™ at School • ©2011 Super Duper® Publications • www.superduperinc.com • 1-800-277-8737   151

Simply Social 7™: Working with Others in a Group

Take-Home Practice

Dear Parent/Helper,

Today we talked about seven steps to follow when working with others in a group called the **Simply Social 7**. Please review these with your child. Have him/her read or repeat the statement in italics that follows each step. Then sign, date, and return this page. We will add this page to your child's *Simply Social Skills Book!*

Here are the **Simply Social 7** for **Working with Others in a Group**…

1. **Choose a leader** – *I will help to choose a leader of the group and consider that the leader may or may not be me.*

2. **Identify who will do each task** – *I will choose a task and know what I am supposed to do.*

3. **Follow instructions** – *I will follow all of the instructions to complete my task.*

4. **Be patient** – *I will not rush others to get their tasks done if I finish mine early.*

5. **Help your teammates** – *I will offer to help my teammates finish their tasks if I finish mine first.*

6. **Stay focused and don't give up** – *I will keep working and let the group leader know if I need help.*

7. **Let others know what you're thinking, but be polite** – *I will share my opinions in a way that will not hurt other people's feelings.*

_____   _____   _____
Parent/Helper Signature   Student Signature   Date

- -

Congratulations!

You are a Simply Social Superstar!

Student Directions: After you return the top of this page to your teacher, cut out the award to the right. Add it to the award page in your *Simply Social Skills Book* or to your award wall in your classroom or at home.

152   #BK-371 Simply Social 7™ at School • ©2011 Super Duper® Publications • www.superduperinc.com • 1-800-277-8737

Accepting "No"

Simply Social 7 Steps

Teacher says: Nobody likes to hear the word, "No." When you want something, "No" can be a very frustrating answer. When a teacher or staff member tells you, "No," there's usually a good reason for it — he/she wants what is best for you, and sometimes, "No" is the best answer.

Directions: Teacher will read the **Simply Social 7** steps. Student(s) will read or repeat the statements in italics that follow.

❶ Ask politely – Remember to use your manners when you ask a question. If you are polite when you ask, the person you're talking to can focus on your question instead of the way you are asking.

I will say, "Please" when I ask my question even if I think the person will tell me, "No."

❷ Wait for a response – Don't be impatient. The person you're speaking to may need some time to think about your question before giving you an answer.

I will wait patiently for the other person to give me an answer.

❸ Listen to what the other person says – If the other person tells you, "No," there may be a good reason for it.

I will listen to everything someone says when he/she gives me an answer.

❹ Don't ask why – The person may not give you a reason for saying, "No" because he/she might be busy or feel that he/she doesn't need to give you a reason.

I will not ask why if someone tells me, "No."

❺ Don't beg! – You may be really frustrated that the other person said, "No," but don't beg him/her to change his/her answer. Begging doesn't usually work, and it may just frustrate the other person.

I will not beg the person to change his/her mind when he/she tells me, "No."

❻ Keep your cool – When someone tells you "No," don't have a temper tantrum. It will not change the other person's mind and will just make both of you unhappy.

I will remain calm, take a deep breath, and count to ten instead of losing my temper.

❼ Think about your other choices – You can't change the other person's mind. So think about what you can do instead.

I will think about what I can do instead if someone tells me, "No."

Accepting "No"

Look and Learn

Teacher says: The students in this scene have been told they didn't win the contest.

Directions: 1. **Draw a circle** around each student who **is accepting, "No."**

2. **Draw an X** on each student who **is not accepting, "No."**

Accepting "No"

Think and Review

Directions: Read the stories, and then answer the questions below about the **Simply Social 7** for Accepting "No."

1. **In the classroom…** Max wanted to have a snack but his teacher told him it was time to take a spelling test. Max took out a pencil and a blank sheet of paper, wrote his name at the top, and prepared to take the test.

    Did Max do the right thing?   a) Yes – What could he do next?

    b) No – What should he have done?

2. **At school…** At lunch Lolita asked a friend if she could have one of his cookies. Her friend didn't want to share. Lolita took a cookie anyway.

    Did Lolita do the right thing?   a) Yes – What could she do next?

    b) No – What should she have done?

3. **At home…** Liam wanted to watch a television program, but his mom told him that he had to do his math homework instead. Liam got out his math book and began his homework.

    Did Liam do the right thing?   a) Yes – What could he do next?

    b) No – What should he have done?

4. **In the community…** Emma asked her mom if they could buy a new cereal she saw in a magazine. Her mom told her they didn't need any cereal right now. Emma threw herself on the ground and begged her mom to buy the cereal.

    Did Emma do the right thing?   a) Yes – What could she do next?

    b) No – What should she have done?

Discussion Questions

1. What are some situations in which you had to accept, "No" for an answer?

2. What would happen if you were told, "Yes" all the time?

Simply Social 7: Accepting "No"

Take-Home Practice

Dear Parent/Helper,

Today we talked about seven steps to follow when accepting "no" called the **Simply Social 7**. Please review these with your child. Have him/her read or repeat the statement in italics that follows each step. Then sign, date, and return this page. We will add this page to your child's *Simply Social Skills Book!*

Here are the **Simply Social 7** for **Accepting "No"**...

1 **Ask politely** – *I will say, "Please" when I ask my question even if I think the person will tell me, "No."*

2 **Wait for a response** – *I will wait patiently for the other person to give me an answer.*

3 **Listen to what the other person says** – *I will listen to everything someone says when he/she gives me an answer.*

4 **Don't ask why** – *I will not ask why if someone tells me, "No."*

5 **Don't beg!** – *I will not beg the person to change his/her mind when he/she tells me, "No."*

6 **Keep your cool** – *I will remain calm, take a deep breath, and count to ten instead of losing my temper.*

7 **Think about your other choices** – *I will think about what I can do instead if someone tells me, "No."*

_____   _____   _____
Parent/Helper Signature   Student Signature   Date

- -

Congratulations!

You are a Simply Social Superstar!

Student Directions: After you return the top of this page to your teacher, cut out the award to the right. Add it to the award page in your *Simply Social Skills Book* or to your award wall in your classroom or at home.

Simply Social 7 — Accepting Consequences

Simply Social 7 Steps

Teacher says: *Consequences* are the events that come after you make choices. Everyone likes the positive consequences that come after making good choices. But it is also important to take responsibility for the poor choices you make so that you can learn and grow.

Directions: Teacher will read the **Simply Social 7** steps. Student(s) will read or repeat the statements in italics that follow.

1 Understand that every choice has consequences – Every choice you make has consequences, either good or bad.

I will think about the consequences before I make a choice.

2 Make your choice – After you think about the consequences of your choice, go ahead and make it.

I will I make a choice and follow through with my decision.

3 Listen to the other person – When you make a choice, someone may tell you if it was a good choice or a poor choice and the consequences. Listen to what he/she has to say. The other person may explain something that you didn't think of before.

I will listen to what other people say about my choice.

4 Don't get angry – It's okay to feel sad when you make a poor choice, but don't get angry with someone else because of a choice you made.

I will not get angry when I make a poor choice.

5 Don't make excuses – Don't blame someone or something else for the decisions you make.

I will take responsibility for the choices I make.

6 Apologize – If you make a choice that hurts someone or made someone feel bad, then you should apologize to him/her.

I will say, "I'm sorry" if my decision hurts someone.

7 Think about what you will do differently next time – Think about whether or not a different choice would have been better. This may help you make a better choice next time.

I will think about what I will do the next time I am in a similar situation.

#BK-371 Simply Social 7™ at School • ©2011 Super Duper® Publications • www.superduperinc.com • 1-800-277-8737

Accepting Consequences

Look and Learn

Teacher says: The students in this scene have made poor choices in their activities around school.

Directions: 1. **Draw a circle** around each student who **is accepting consequences**.

2. **Draw an X** on each student who **is not accepting consequences**.

Simply Social 7 — Accepting Consequences

Think and Review

Directions: Read the stories, and then answer the questions below about the **Simply Social 7** for **Accepting Consequences**.

1. **In the classroom...** Ella went to the movies instead of studying for her history test. She got a poor grade on the test. Ella told the teacher that it wasn't her fault because she was really sick and wasn't able to study.

   Did Ella do the right thing?   a) Yes – What could she do next?

   b) No – What should she have done?

2. **At school...** Javier was horsing around at lunch and spilled his milk. The lunch monitor told him he had to eat at a separate table the next day. The next day, without being told, Javier took his lunch to a separate table to eat.

   Did Javier do the right thing?   a) Yes – What could he do next?

   b) No – What should he have done?

3. **At home...** Ava's mom asked her to be ready to go to the play at seven o'clock. Instead Ava talked to her friend on the phone. Ava and her mom missed the first act of the play. Ava blamed her mom for driving too slowly.

   Did Ava do the right thing?   a) Yes – What could she do next?

   b) No – What should she have done?

4. **In the community...** Jaden dove into the shallow end of the pool even though there were "No Diving" signs posted at the shallow end. The lifeguard told Jaden that he had to leave. Jaden apologized to the lifeguard, picked up his belongings, and went home.

   Did Jaden do the right thing?   a) Yes – What could he do next?

   b) No – What should he have done?

Discussion Questions

1. What are some situations in which you had to accept the consequences of your actions?

2. What would happen if there were no consequences for your actions?

#BK-371 Simply Social 7™ at School • ©2011 Super Duper® Publications • www.superduperinc.com • 1-800-277-8737

Simply Social 7: Accepting Consequences

Take-Home Practice

Dear Parent/Helper,

Today we talked about seven steps to follow when accepting consequences called the **Simply Social 7**. Please review these with your child. Have him/her read or repeat the statement in italics that follows each step. Then sign, date, and return this page. We will add this page to your child's *Simply Social Skills Book!*

Here are the **Simply Social 7** for **Accepting Consequences**...

1. **Understand that every choice has consequences** – *I will think about the consequences before I make a choice.*

2. **Make your choice** – *I will make a choice and follow through with my decision.*

3. **Listen to the other person** – *I will listen to what other people say about my choice.*

4. **Don't get angry** – *I will not get angry when I make a poor choice.*

5. **Don't make excuses** – *I will take responsibility for the choices I make.*

6. **Apologize** – *I will say, "I'm sorry" if my decision hurts someone.*

7. **Think about what you will do differently next time** – *I will think about what I will do the next time I am in a similar situation.*

_____   _____   _____
Parent/Helper Signature   Student Signature   Date

- -

Congratulations!

You are a Simply Social Superstar!

Student Directions: After you return the top of this page to your teacher, cut out the award to the right. Add it to the award page in your *Simply Social Skills Book* or to your award wall in your classroom or at home.

160   #BK-371 Simply Social 7™ at School • ©2011 Super Duper® Publications • www.superduperinc.com • 1-800-277-8737

Simply Social 7 — Accepting Discipline

Simply Social 7 Steps

Teacher says: *Discipline* is another word for punishment. When we misbehave or break the rules we receive discipline for our actions. Discipline helps us learn what we did wrong so that we can change our behavior. In school a teacher may discipline you for behavior like talking out of turn, running in the hallway, or hurting other students.

Directions: Teacher will read the **Simply Social 7** steps. Student(s) will read or repeat the statements in italics that follow.

1 **Know that rules exist for a reason** – Rules keep us safe and help us treat each other fairly. When you break a rule, you could hurt yourself or someone else.

I will remember that rules are important.

2 **Listen to what the adult says** – You may be upset when you get in trouble, but listen to what the adult says. The adult will tell you what you did wrong and can help you understand why it matters.

I will listen to what the adult tells me about what I did wrong.

3 **Realize that you can learn from discipline** – Discipline helps you understand the poor choices you make so can change your behavior.

I will learn from my mistakes.

4 **Keep your cool** – Don't get angry and lash out at others just because you got in trouble. Anger will only add to your unhappiness.

I will remain calm when I am disciplined.

5 **Don't talk back** – Talking back to an adult is disrespectful and can lead to more discipline.

I will not argue nor talk back to an adult when I am being disciplined.

6 **Apologize for your behavior** – Once you understand the mistake you made and why it was inappropriate, apologize to the person(s) you hurt or upset.

I will say I am sorry for my behavior.

7 **Decide how you will change your behavior in the future** – Think about what you can do differently the next time you're in a similar situation.

*I will think about how to change my behavior the next time
I find myself in a similar situation.*

#BK-371 Simply Social 7™ at School • ©2011 Super Duper® Publications • www.superduperinc.com • 1-800-277-8737   161

Accepting Discipline

Look and Learn

Teacher says: The students in this scene are receiving discipline for their actions at school.

Directions: 1. **Draw a circle** around each student who **is accepting discipline**.

2. **Draw an X** on each student who **is not accepting discipline**.

Simply Social 7™

Accepting Discipline

Think and Review

Directions: Read the stories, and then answer the questions below about the **Simply Social 7** for **Accepting Discipline**.

1. **In the classroom…** Mario's teacher caught him talking to another student during a test. The teacher told Mario to turn in his test. Mario ignored the teacher and kept working.

   Did Mario do the right thing?

   a) Yes – What could he do next?

   b) No – What should he have done?

2. **At school…** A teacher caught Aurora on her cell phone between classes. Using a cell phone at school is not allowed, so the teacher told Aurora to give him her cell phone. Aurora apologized and handed her phone to the teacher.

   Did Aurora do the right thing?

   a) Yes – What could she do next?

   b) No – What should she have done?

3. **At home…** Dylan got in trouble for lying to his parents. His parents told him not to play video games for a week. After Dylan's parents went to bed, Dylan sneaked out of his room to play video games.

   Did Dylan do the right thing?

   a) Yes – What could he do next?

   b) No – What should he have done?

4. **In the community…** Isabella went to the zoo with her brother. She ignored the "Do not feed the animals" sign and gave food to the monkeys. A zookeeper told her she had to leave the exhibit. Isabella got mad and threw her trash on the ground.

   Did Isabella do the right thing?

   a) Yes – What could she do next?

   b) No – What should she have done?

Discussion Questions

1. What are some situations in which you had to accept discipline for your actions?

2. What would happen if nobody disciplined you when you misbehaved or didn't follow the rules?

#BK-371 Simply Social 7™ at School • ©2011 Super Duper® Publications • www.superduperinc.com • 1-800-277-8737
163

Simply Social 7: Accepting Discipline

Take-Home Practice

Dear Parent/Helper,

Today we talked about seven steps to follow when accepting discipline called the **Simply Social 7**. Please review these with your child. Have him/her read or repeat the statement in italics that follows each step. Then sign, date, and return this page. We will add this page to your child's *Simply Social Skills Book!*

Here are the **Simply Social 7** for **Accepting Discipline**…

❶ Know that rules exist for a reason – *I will remember that rules are important.*

❷ Listen to what the adult says – *I will listen to what the adult tells me about what I did wrong.*

❸ Realize that you can learn from discipline – *I will learn from my mistakes.*

❹ Keep your cool – *I will remain calm when I am disciplined.*

❺ Don't talk back – *I will not argue nor talk back to an adult when I am being disciplined.*

❻ Apologize for your behavior – *I will say I am sorry for my behavior.*

❼ Decide how you will change your behavior in the future – *I will think about how to change my behavior the next time I find myself in a similar situation.*

_____   _____   _____
Parent/Helper Signature   Student Signature   Date

 -

Congratulations!
You are a Simply Social Superstar!

Student Directions: After you return the top of this page to your teacher, cut out the award to the right. Add it to the award page in your *Simply Social Skills Book* or to your award wall in your classroom or at home.

Simply Social 7 — Accepting Constructive Criticism

Simply Social 7 Steps

Teacher says: *Constructive criticism* is the advice people give you to help improve your work. Teachers use constructive criticism to help you. For example, when you turn in your work at school the teacher may give it back with comments about what you did well and what you could have done better.

Directions: Teacher will read the **Simply Social 7** steps. Student(s) will read or repeat the statements in italics that follow.

1 **Remember that nobody is perfect** – Everybody makes mistakes and everyone will receive constructive criticism throughout his/her life.

I will remember that it is okay to make mistakes.

2 **Look at constructive criticism as a good thing** – Constructive criticism may seem harsh, but it can actually help you see what you did wrong and what you can do better next time.

I will look for the positives in constructive criticism.

3 **Listen to constructive criticism** – Listen to what the other person has to say so you will know how to improve your work.

I will listen to the other person so that I can learn from my mistakes.

4 **Try to leave your emotions out** – Remember that the other person is criticizing your work or your actions — not you as a person.

I will not get upset when someone criticizes my work or actions.

5 **Wait before you react** – Your instant reaction might be anger, but give yourself time to think about your response before you react.

I will take a deep breath, count to five, and think about my response before I react.

6 **Look for the usefulness of constructive criticism** – After listening to constructive criticism, decide if there was something you could have done better.

*I will remember the helpful parts of the criticism so
that I can improve my work or actions.*

7 **Don't hold a grudge** – After you receive constructive criticism and learn from your mistakes, let it go! If you remain upset, it can ruin the rest of your day and make it difficult to do your best on the activities that follow.

I will learn from the constructive criticism I receive, and then I will move on!

#BK-371 Simply Social 7™ at School • ©2011 Super Duper® Publications • www.superduperinc.com • 1-800-277-8737

Simply Social 7 — Accepting Constructive Criticism

Look and Learn

Teacher says: The students in this scene have received constructive criticism from their art teacher.

Directions: 1. **Draw a circle** around each student who **is accepting constructive criticism**.

2. **Draw an X** on each student who **is not accepting constructive criticism**.

Simply Social 7™ Accepting Constructive Criticism

Think and Review

Directions: Read the stories, and then answer the questions below about the **Simply Social 7** for **Accepting Constructive Criticism**.

1. **In the classroom...** Adriana got her graded essay back with written comments on it from her teacher. She read the comments and used her teacher's suggestions the next time she wrote an essay.

   Did Adriana do the right thing?   a) Yes – What could she do next?

   b) No – What should she have done?

2. **At school...** Ethan's occupational therapist gave him a suggestion on how to hold his scissors properly. Ethan got mad and threw the scissors across the room.

   Did Ethan do the right thing?   a) Yes – What could he do next?

   b) No – What should he have done?

3. **At home...** Jack's sister told him that his new haircut was too short. Jack got upset and told his sister that she was wearing an ugly dress.

   Did Jack do the right thing?   a) Yes – What could he do next?

   b) No – What should he have done?

4. **In the community...** The postal worker told Genevieve that the letter she was mailing might be delayed because the address she wrote was difficult to read. Genevieve re-wrote the address using neater handwriting.

   Did Genevieve do the right thing?   a) Yes – What could she do next?

   b) No – What should she have done?

Discussion Questions

1. What are some situations in which you had to accept constructive criticism?

2. What would happen if no one offered constructive criticism on your work or actions?

#BK-371 Simply Social 7™ at School • ©2011 Super Duper® Publications • www.superduperinc.com • 1-800-277-8737   167

Simply Social 7: Accepting Constructive Criticism

Take-Home Practice

Dear Parent/Helper,

Today we talked about seven steps to follow when accepting constructive criticism called the **Simply Social 7**. Please review these with your child. Have him/her read or repeat the statement in italics that follows each step. Then sign, date, and return this page. We will add this page to your child's *Simply Social Skills Book!*

Here are the **Simply Social 7** for **Accepting Constructive Criticism**…

1. **Remember that nobody is perfect** – *I will remember that it is okay to make mistakes.*

2. **Look at constructive criticism as a good thing** – *I will look for the positives in constructive criticism.*

3. **Listen to constructive criticism** – *I will listen to the other person so that I can learn from my mistakes.*

4. **Try to leave your emotions out** – *I will not get upset when someone criticizes my work or actions.*

5. **Wait before you react** – *I will take a deep breath, count to five, and think about my response before I react.*

6. **Look for the usefulness of constructive criticism** – *I will remember the helpful parts of the criticism so that I can improve my work or actions.*

7. **Don't hold a grudge** – *I will learn from the constructive criticism I receive, and then I will move on!*

_____   _____   _____
Parent/Helper Signature   Student Signature   Date

- -

Congratulations!

You are a Simply Social Superstar!

Student Directions: After you return the top of this page to your teacher, cut out the award to the right. Add it to the award page in your *Simply Social Skills Book* or to your award wall in your classroom or at home.

Simply Social 7 | Dealing with Failure

Simply Social 7 Steps

Teacher says: Have you ever done poorly on a test or not put 100 percent of your effort into an assignment? Getting a bad grade can make you feel pretty low. But when you fail at something it doesn't mean you aren't smart, or that you're going to fail at everything. It just means you still have more to learn.

Directions: Teacher will read the **Simply Social 7** steps. Student(s) will read or repeat the statements in italics that follow.

1 **Don't beat yourself up** – Failure happens to everyone. Don't be hard on yourself.

I will remember that it is okay to experience failure as long as I learn from it.

2 **Don't make excuses** – When you blame your failure on something else it prevents you from learning from your mistakes.

I will take responsibility for a failure so that I can learn from it.

3 **Try to leave your emotions out** – When your emotions get involved it becomes more difficult to think clearly.

I will try to remain calm when dealing with failure.

4 **Identify what went wrong** – Figure out what led to the failure so you can do things differently the next time you're in a similar situation.

I will discover what I did wrong so that I will be successful next time.

5 **Decide what you can do differently next time** – Once you know what went wrong, decide what you will change next time.

I will decide what to do the next time I am in a similar situation.

6 **Move on** – Don't continue to think about the failure. Dwelling on a failure will only keep you from doing your best on the next task.

I will not continue to think about the failure after
I have identified what I will do differently next time.

7 **Try again** – We only really fail when we quit.

I will not give up! I will learn from my mistakes, and I will keep trying!

#BK-371 Simply Social 7™ at School • ©2011 Super Duper® Publications • www.superduperinc.com • 1-800-277-8737

Dealing with Failure

Look and Learn

Teacher says: The students in this scene are struggling with basketball.

Directions: 1. **Draw a circle** around each student who **is dealing with failure** appropriately.

2. **Draw an X** on each student who **is not dealing with failure** appropriately.

Simply Social 7 — Dealing with Failure

Think and Review

Directions: Read the stories, and then answer the questions below about the **Simply Social 7** for **Dealing with Failure**.

1. **In the classroom...** Connor did his homework on the bus ride to school. When he got an *F* on the assignment he decided from then on to do his homework the night before so that he would have more time.

   Did Connor do the right thing?   a) Yes – What could he do next?

   b) No – What should he have done?

2. **At school...** Lorelei was playing basketball with her class. Every time she tried to get the ball in the net, she missed. She decided that with some extra practice her aim would improve.

   Did Lorelei do the right thing?   a) Yes – What could she do next?

   b) No – What should she have done?

3. **At home...** Noah was building a tree house in the backyard. When he used a hammer to hang a poster on the wall the roof caved in. Noah got mad and started hitting the walls and floor with the hammer.

   Did Noah do the right thing?   a) Yes – What could he do next?

   b) No – What should he have done?

4. **In the community...** Belle was looking for a shoe store at the mall. She used the mall's directory to see where the store was. When she arrived at the location where the store should be she realized she read the directory wrong. Belle went back to the directory to try again.

   Did Belle do the right thing?   a) Yes – What could she do next?

   b) No – What should she have done?

Discussion Questions

1. What are some situations in which you had to deal with failure?

2. What would happen if you gave up every time you experienced failure?

#BK-371 Simply Social 7™ at School • ©2011 Super Duper® Publications • www.superduperinc.com • 1-800-277-8737

Simply Social 7 — Dealing with Failure

Take-Home Practice

Dear Parent/Helper,

Today we talked about seven steps to follow when dealing with failure called the **Simply Social 7**. Please review these with your child. Have him/her read or repeat the statement in italics that follows each step. Then sign, date, and return this page. We will add this page to your child's *Simply Social Skills Book!*

Here are the **Simply Social 7** for **Dealing with Failure**…

❶ **Don't beat yourself up** – *I will remember that it is okay to experience failure as long as I learn from it.*

❷ **Don't make excuses** – *I will take responsibility for a failure so that I can learn from it.*

❸ **Try to leave your emotions out** – *I will try to remain calm when dealing with failure.*

❹ **Identify what went wrong** – *I will discover what I did wrong so that I will be successful next time.*

❺ **Decide what you can do differently next time** – *I will decide what to do the next time I am in a similar situation.*

❻ **Move on** – *I will not continue to think about the failure after I have identified what I will do differently next time.*

❼ **Try again** – *I will not give up! I will learn from my mistakes, and I will keep trying!*

_____   _____   _____
Parent/Helper Signature   Student Signature   Date

- -

Congratulations!

You are a Simply Social Superstar!

Student Directions: After you return the top of this page to your teacher, cut out the award to the right. Add it to the award page in your *Simply Social Skills Book* or to your award wall in your classroom or at home.

Simply Social 7 — Resolving Conflict

Simply Social 7 Steps

Teacher says: We all have different thoughts and ideas about certain subjects. *Conflict* often occurs when people disagree with one another and get into an argument over those differences. Conflict may be uncomfortable, but it is not always bad. Conflict can help us learn and grow when we work together to find a solution to the problem.

Directions: Teacher will read the **Simply Social 7** steps. Student(s) will read or repeat the statements in italics that follow.

1 **Stay calm** – It is difficult to think clearly and communicate logically when you are angry and frustrated.

I will remain calm when conflict arises. I will take a deep breath and count to ten if I need to settle down.

2 **Remain respectful** – Even if you disagree with someone's ideas or opinions, there is no need to be rude or impolite.

I will continue to be considerate of the other person's feelings, even when I disagree with him/her.

3 **Discuss the situation** – Remember there are two parts to a discussion—speaking and listening. Share your thoughts about the situation, but take time to listen to the other person's thoughts and feelings.

I will tell the other person what I think, but I will also listen to what he/she has to say.

4 **Work together to create a solution** – In order to resolve the conflict both sides may have to give a little. This is called *compromise*.

I will work with the other person to find a solution to the conflict that both of us can benefit from.

5 **Ask someone else** – If you are not able to resolve the conflict by yourselves, talk to someone who is not involved in the situation. He/She may be able to see a solution to the conflict that is fair for both sides.

I will suggest we ask for help from someone who is not involved in the conflict if we cannot find a solution.

6 **Accept the solution** – When both sides have worked together to find a solution to the conflict, agree to it.

I will accept the solution that we have agreed upon.

7 **Let it go** – After you find a solution don't continue to think about who was right or wrong. Doing so will just damage the relationship between you and the other person.

I will move on and not think about the conflict anymore.

#BK-371 Simply Social 7™ at School • ©2011 Super Duper® Publications • www.superduperinc.com • 1-800-277-8737

Resolving Conflict

Look and Learn

Teacher says: The students in this scene are involved in conflict with other students during a baseball game.

Directions: 1. **Draw a circle** around each student who **is resolving conflict** appropriately.

2. **Draw an X** on each student who **is not resolving conflict** appropriately.

Simply Social 7

Resolving Conflict

Think and Review

Directions: Read the stories, and then answer the questions below about the **Simply Social 7** for **Resolving Conflict.**

1. **In the classroom...** Martin wanted to use a glass bottle as part of a class experiment because it was sturdier than plastic. His classmate wanted to use a plastic bottle because it wouldn't break. After a discussion about the experiment they both agreed to use a metal can because it was sturdy and wouldn't break.

   Did Martin do the right thing?   a) Yes – What could he do next?

                                          b) No – What should he have done?

2. **At school...** While planning the spring dance Chelsea and another classmate got into an argument over decorations. Chelsea thought her classmate's idea to have balloons instead of streamers was silly and decided she wouldn't speak to her classmate anymore.

   Did Chelsea do the right thing?   a) Yes – What could she do next?

                                          b) No – What should she have done?

3. **At home...** It was family movie night and Sydney and her brother wanted to watch different movies. Sydney offered to watch her brother's movie this time if she could choose the movie for the next two movie nights.

   Did Sydney do the right thing?   a) Yes – What could she do next?

                                          b) No – What should she have done?

4. **In the community...** Wyatt's friend wanted to order a pizza with pepperoni. Wyatt only wanted sausage on his pizza. When Wyatt's friend suggested they order a pizza with half pepperoni and half sausage, Wyatt argued that he didn't want any pepperoni on the pizza.

   Did Wyatt do the right thing?   a) Yes – What could he do next?

                                          b) No – What should he have done?

Discussion Questions

1. What are some situations in which you were able to resolve conflict?

2. What would happen if no one ever tried to resolve conflict?

#BK-371 Simply Social 7™ at School • ©2011 Super Duper® Publications • www.superduperinc.com • 1-800-277-8737   175

Simply Social 7: Resolving Conflict

Take-Home Practice

Dear Parent/Helper,

Today we talked about seven steps to follow when resolving conflict called the **Simply Social 7**. Please review these with your child. Have him/her read or repeat the statement in italics that follows each step. Then sign, date, and return this page. We will add this page to your child's *Simply Social Skills Book!*

Here are the **Simply Social 7** for **Resolving Conflict**...

1 **Stay calm** – *I will remain calm when conflict arises. I will take a deep breath and count to ten if I need to settle down.*

2 **Remain respectful** – *I will continue to be considerate of the other person's feelings, even when I disagree with him/her.*

3 **Discuss the situation** – *I will tell the other person what I think, but I will also listen to what he/she has to say.*

4 **Work together to create a solution** – *I will work with the other person to find a solution to the conflict that both of us can benefit from.*

5 **Ask someone else** – *I will suggest we ask for help from someone who is not involved in the conflict if we cannot find a solution.*

6 **Accept the solution** – *I will accept the solution that we have agree upon.*

7 **Let it go** – *I will move on and not think about the conflict anymore.*

_____   _____   _____
Parent/Helper Signature   Student Signature   Date

- -

Congratulations!

You are a Simply Social Superstar!

Student Directions: After you return the top of this page to your teacher, cut out the award to the right. Add it to the award page in your *Simply Social Skills Book* or to your award wall in your classroom or at home.

Simply Social 7 | Understanding Facial Expressions

Simply Social 7 Steps

Teacher says: Sometimes other people know when you are happy, sad, angry, surprised, or excited just by looking at your face. *Facial expressions* are made by the movements of the muscles in your face. The curve of your mouth, twinkle of your eye, and movement of your eyebrows all have a part in how your facial expressions are interpreted by others.

Directions: Teacher will read the **Simply Social 7** steps. Student(s) will read or repeat the statements in italics that follow.

1 **Remember that facial expressions can communicate information without words** – Your facial expressions and other nonverbal signals are as important as the words you say.

I will remember that facial expressions are just as important as words when communicating with others.

2 **Remember that facial expressions are automatic** – Facial expressions are usually involuntary. This means that they often happen without thinking about them.

I will remember that people often use facial expressions without thinking about them.

3 **Look in the mirror** – Practice different facial expressions in your mirror at home. What do you have to change in order to look happy? Sad? Angry? Surprised? Excited?

I will use a mirror to practice different facial expressions.

4 **Try drawing different facial expressions** – Drawing cartoon faces with different facial expressions can help you explore the facial features that make us look like we feel one way or another.

I will try drawing different faces to explore the facial features that determine our expressions.

5 **Look at people when you are speaking to them** – It is important to look at people when they are speaking. Not only is it polite, but it will help you interpret their facial expressions.

I will look at people's faces so I can see their expressions.

6 **Observe the facial expressions of others** – Look at the faces of other people around you. Try to determine how they are feeling by the expressions on their faces.

I will watch people's faces and determine how they feel based on their facial expressions.

7 **Understand that sometimes facial expressions are used to indicate sarcasm** – When someone's facial expression gives the opposite idea of what he/she is saying, it might mean that he/she is using sarcasm.

I will remember when someone's words do not match his/her facial expressions, he/she could be using sarcasm.

#BK-371 Simply Social 7™ at School • ©2011 Super Duper® Publications • www.superduperinc.com • 1-800-277-8737

177

Understanding Facial Expressions

Look and Learn

Teacher says: The students in this scene are responding to their classmates' facial expressions.

Directions: 1. **Draw a circle** around each student who **is understanding facial expressions**.

2. **Draw an X** on each student who **is not understanding facial expressions**.

Simply Social 7 · Understanding Facial Expressions

Think and Review

Directions: Read the stories, and then answer the questions below about the **Simply Social 7** for **Understanding Facial Expressions**.

1. **In the classroom...** After the math test Ashley smiled at her friend and said, "I think I got the wrong answer on every question!" Ashley's friend thought she was happy about failing the math test.

   Did Ashley do the right thing?   a) Yes – What could she do next?

   b) No – What should she have done?

2. **At school...** During baseball practice Alexander hit his teammate with the ball by accident. Alexander could tell his teammate was angry because of the look on his face, so he apologized to his teammate.

   Did Alexander do the right thing?   a) Yes – What could he do next?

   b) No – What should he have done?

3. **At home...** Brianna's mom told her they were going on vacation to see her grandmother. Brianna could tell her mom was excited to see her grandmother because she was talking about the vacation with bright eyes and a smile on her face.

   Did Brianna do the right thing?   a) Yes – What could she do next?

   b) No – What should she have done?

4. **In the community...** While playing in the park Reginald's friend said he was very excited about going to the zoo with his little brother. Reginald wasn't looking at his friend when he was speaking, so he didn't know if his friend was being serious or sarcastic.

   Did Reginald do the right thing?   a) Yes – What could he do next?

   b) No – What should he have done?

Discussion Questions

1. What are some situations in which you have seen facial expressions being used?

2. What would happen if you walked around all day with a forced smile on your face?

#BK-371 Simply Social 7™ at School • ©2011 Super Duper® Publications • www.superduperinc.com • 1-800-277-8737   179

Simply Social 7: Understanding Facial Expressions

Take-Home Practice

Dear Parent/Helper,

Today we talked about seven steps to follow when understanding facial expressions called the **Simply Social 7**. Please review these with your child. Have him/her read or repeat the statement in italics that follows each step. Then sign, date, and return this page. We will add this page to your child's *Simply Social Skills Book!*

Here are the **Simply Social 7** for **Understanding Facial Expressions**...

1. **Remember that facial expressions can communicate information without words** – *I will remember that facial expressions are just as important as words when communicating with others.*

2. **Remember that facial expressions are automatic** – *I will remember that people often use facial expressions without thinking about them.*

3. **Look in the mirror** – *I will use a mirror to practice different facial expressions.*

4. **Try drawing different facial expressions** – *I will try drawing different faces to explore the facial features that determine our expressions.*

5. **Look at people when you are speaking to them** – *I will look at people's faces so I can see their expressions.*

6. **Observe the facial expressions of others** – *I will watch people's faces and determine how they feel based on their facial expressions.*

7. **Understand that sometimes facial expressions are used to indicate sarcasm** – *I will remember when someone's words do not match his/her facial expressions, he/she could be using sarcasm.*

_____   _____   _____
Parent/Helper Signature   Student Signature   Date

- -

Congratulations!

You are a Simply Social Superstar!

Student Directions: After you return the top of this page to your teacher, cut out the award to the right. Add it to the award page in your *Simply Social Skills Book* or to your award wall in your classroom or at home.

180   #BK-371 Simply Social 7™ at School • ©2011 Super Duper® Publications • www.superduperinc.com • 1-800-277-8737

Simply Social 7 — Understanding Emotions

Simply Social 7 Steps

Teacher says: Your *emotions* are an indication of how you feel about a situation. When something makes you angry, happy, or scared, you typically feel it before you have time to stop and think about it. You must be able to understand your emotions in order to respond appropriately to the situations that cause them.

Directions: Teacher will read the **Simply Social 7** steps. Student(s) will read or repeat the statements in italics that follow.

1 **Know that emotions are okay** – Emotions and feelings are natural. Everybody has them.

I will remember that everyone has emotions and it is okay to have them.

2 **Observe others** – Learn about emotions by looking at other people. Use what you see to try to determine which emotions they are experiencing.

I will observe others to learn how to recognize emotions.

3 **Pay attention to facial expressions** – We can often tell which emotion others are feeling based on the curve of their mouths, look in their eyes, and movement of their eyebrows.

I will look at people's facial expressions to help me understand which emotions they are experiencing.

4 **Recognize how emotions affect posture** – Your posture is affected by the emotions you are feeling. For example, someone with drooping shoulders may be sad, while someone who is standing up straight may be happy.

I will remember that posture can provide clues about the emotions people are experiencing.

5 **Examine the situation** – Look at the events leading up to the emotional experience. What happened to make you feel the way you do?

I will look at my situation to help me understand the emotions I am experiencing.

6 **Don't be afraid to show your emotions** – Expressing your emotions is healthy and natural.

I will not be afraid to show my emotions.

7 **Find appropriate ways to release your emotions** – It is not healthy to keep your emotions bottled up inside of you. However, emotions should be expressed in ways that are helpful and not hurtful to others.

I will express my emotions in ways that are helpful and not hurtful to others.

#BK-371 Simply Social 7™ at School • ©2011 Super Duper® Publications • www.superduperinc.com • 1-800-277-8737

181

Understanding Emotions

Look and Learn

Teacher says: The students in this scene are experiencing different emotions.

Directions: 1. **Draw a circle** around each student who **is understanding emotions**.

2. **Draw an X** on each student who **is not understanding emotions**.

Simply Social 7 — Understanding Emotions

Think and Review

Directions: Read the stories, and then answer the questions below about the **Simply Social 7** for **Understanding Emotions**.

1. **In the classroom…** After the pop quiz Brody noticed his friend's shoulders were drooping and the corners of his mouth were turned down. Brody approached his friend and congratulated him for doing well on the pop quiz.

   Did Brody do the right thing?   a) Yes – What could he do next?

   b) No – What should he have done?

2. **At school…** Jocelyn was disappointed that she didn't make the track team at school. When her friend asked how the tryouts went Jocelyn yelled at her friend for bringing up an unhappy subject.

   Did Jocelyn do the right thing?   a) Yes – What could she do next?

   b) No – What should she have done?

3. **At home…** Zoe's sister borrowed her favorite sweater without asking and got a stain on it. Zoe was really angry that her sister ruined her sweater but instead of yelling at his sister she went outside and dribbled a basketball.

   Did Zoe do the right thing?   a) Yes – What could she do next?

   b) No – What should she have done?

4. **In the community…** Garrett went to the aquarium with his friends. Seeing the fish in the tanks reminded him of the pet fish he lost the week before and tears welled up in his eyes. When his friends asked if he was okay, Garrett tried to hide his tears and said, "Of course I'm fine!"

   Did Garrett do the right thing?   a) Yes – What could he do next?

   b) No – What should he have done?

Discussion Questions

1. What are some situations in which you had to understand emotions?

2. What would happen if we never released our emotions?

#BK-371 Simply Social 7™ at School • ©2011 Super Duper® Publications • www.superduperinc.com • 1-800-277-8737   183

Simply Social 7: Understanding Emotions

Take-Home Practice

Dear Parent/Helper,

Today we talked about seven steps to follow when understanding emotions called the **Simply Social 7**. Please review these with your child. Have him/her read or repeat the statement in italics that follows each step. Then sign, date, and return this page. We will add this page to your child's *Simply Social Skills Book!*

Here are the **Simply Social 7** for **Understanding Emotions**…

1. **Know that emotions are okay** – *I will remember that everyone has emotions and it is okay to have them.*

2. **Observe others** – *I will observe others to learn how to recognize emotions.*

3. **Pay attention to facial expressions** – *I will look at people's facial expressions to help me understand which emotions they are experiencing.*

4. **Recognize how emotions affect posture** – *I will remember that posture can provide clues about the emotions people are experiencing.*

5. **Examine the situation** – *I will look at my situation to help me understand the emotions I am experiencing.*

6. **Don't be afraid to show your emotions** – *I will not be afraid to show my emotions.*

7. **Find appropriate ways to release your emotions** – *I will express my emotions in ways that are helpful and not hurtful to others.*

_____   _____   _____
Parent/Helper Signature   Student Signature   Date

- -

Congratulations!
You are a Simply Social Superstar!

Student Directions: After you return the top of this page to your teacher, cut out the award to the right. Add it to the award page in your *Simply Social Skills Book* or to your award wall in your classroom or at home.

184   #BK-371 Simply Social 7™ at School • ©2011 Super Duper® Publications • www.superduperinc.com • 1-800-277-8737

Simply Social 7 Steps

Teacher says: Everybody has feelings and emotions. Our feelings help us to know when things are going well or when there is a problem. One of the most difficult things about having feelings is learning to express them in ways that are helpful and not hurtful to others.

Directions: Teacher will read the **Simply Social 7** steps. Student(s) will read or repeat the statements in italics that follow.

1 **Don't keep it bottled up** – It's not healthy to keep your feelings and emotions bottled up inside you.

I will express my feelings in an appropriate way.

2 **Express both positive and negative feelings** – It is healthy to express your feelings, whether positive or negative.

I will tell someone if I am happy, excited, frustrated, or mad.

3 **Use "I" statements instead of "you" statements** – "You" statements blame other people. When people feel like they are being blamed they stop listening and start thinking about how to defend themselves.

I will use "I" statements such as, "When this happened, I felt..."
instead of blaming others.

4 **Be specific about how you feel** – If you tell someone you feel "bad," he/she won't know if you feel sick, tired, sad, or angry.

I will avoid using words like "good" or "bad." I will use specific
words that let the other person know exactly how I am feeling.

5 **State what happened to make you feel that way** – Telling someone what happened to make you feel the way you do can help him/her understand your feelings.

I will explain what happened to make me feel the way I feel.

6 **Don't attack another person** – Even if someone has done something that upsets you, don't yell at him/her.

I will wait until I have settled down before talking about an emotional situation.

7 **If talking is difficult, draw a picture** – Drawing a picture can help you communicate how you feel without having to put it into words.

I will draw a picture about how I feel if talking about it is too difficult.

#BK-371 Simply Social 7™ at School • ©2011 Super Duper® Publications • www.superduperinc.com • 1-800-277-8737

Expressing Feelings

Look and Learn

Teacher says: The students in this scene are experiencing different feelings.

Directions: 1. **Draw a circle** around each student who **is expressing feelings** appropriately.

2. **Draw an X** on each student who **is not expressing feelings** appropriately.

Simply Social 7 — Expressing Feelings

Think and Review

Directions: Read the stories, and then answer the questions below about the **Simply Social 7** for **Expressing Feelings.**

1. **In the classroom...** Caroline left her backpack and homework at home. When her teacher collected the homework assignments, Caroline was so mad she forgot hers that she shoved the chair in front of her and knocked over the person who was sitting in it.

   Did Caroline do the right thing?　　a) Yes – What could she do next?

   　　　　　　　　　　　　　　　　　b) No – What should she have done?

2. **At school...** Jackson was asked to speak at an assembly about recycling. Jackson was nervous about speaking in front of the school, but didn't tell anyone that he was too scared to do it. On the day of the assembly Jackson threw up before going on stage.

   Did Jackson do the right thing?　　a) Yes – What could he do next?

   　　　　　　　　　　　　　　　　　b) No – What should he have done?

3. **At home...** Madison's brothers were playing football inside the house. One of her brothers accidentally threw the ball at Madison's favorite porcelain doll and broke it. Madison told her brother, "When my doll broke, I felt very sad."

   Did Madison do the right thing?　　a) Yes – What could she do next?

   　　　　　　　　　　　　　　　　　b) No – What should she have done?

4. **In the community...** Alexander received a citizenship award for calling 9-1-1 when he saw smoke coming from a neighbor's house. Alexander felt proud about receiving the award and called his friend to tell him about it.

   Did Alexander do the right thing?　　a) Yes – What could he do next?

   　　　　　　　　　　　　　　　　　b) No – What should he have done?

Discussion Questions

1. What are some situations in which you had to express your feelings?

2. What would happen if you expressed only negative feelings all of the time?

#BK-371 Simply Social 7™ at School • ©2011 Super Duper® Publications • www.superduperinc.com • 1-800-277-8737

Simply Social 7: Expressing Feelings

Take-Home Practice

Dear Parent/Helper,

Today we talked about seven steps to follow when expressing feelings called the **Simply Social 7**. Please review these with your child. Have him/her read or repeat the statement in italics that follows each step. Then sign, date, and return this page. We will add this page to your child's *Simply Social Skills Book!*

Here are the **Simply Social 7** for **Expressing Feelings**...

1. **Don't keep it bottled up** – *I will express my feelings in an appropriate way.*

2. **Express both positive and negative feelings** – *I will tell someone if I am happy, excited, frustrated, or mad.*

3. **Use "I" statements instead of "you" statements** – *I will use "I" statements such as, "When this happened, I felt..." instead of blaming others.*

4. **Be specific about how you feel** – *I will avoid using words like "good" or "bad." I will use specific words that let the other person know exactly how I am feeling.*

5. **State what happened to make you feel that way** – *I will explain what happened to make me feel the way I feel.*

6. **Don't attack another person** – *If I am very emotional about a situation, I will wait until I have settled down before talking about an emotional situation.*

7. **If talking is difficult, draw a picture** – *I will draw a picture about how I feel if talking about it is too difficult.*

_____ _____ _____
Parent/Helper Signature   Student Signature   Date

- -

Congratulations!

You are a Simply Social Superstar!

Student Directions: After you return the top of this page to your teacher, cut out the award to the right. Add it to the award page in your *Simply Social Skills Book* or to your award wall in your classroom or at home.

Simply Social 7 — Dealing with Anger

Simply Social 7 Steps

Teacher says: Have you ever been so angry that you wanted to scream? Everybody gets angry sometimes. There's nothing wrong with getting angry, but it's important to deal with your anger in an appropriate and positive way. Screaming is not an appropriate or positive way to deal with anger.

Directions: Teacher will read the **Simply Social 7** steps. Student(s) will read or repeat the statements in italics that follow.

1 Recognize that you are angry – It's important to know that you are angry before you react to the anger.

I will learn to recognize when I am angry so that I will be able to respond appropriately.

2 Take a deep breath – Taking a deep breath can help you calm down.

I will take a deep breath in and let the air out slowly.

3 Count to ten – Counting to ten before you say anything gives you a chance to think about what you are going to say.

I will count to ten and think about how I can calmly talk about the situation.

4 Tell yourself to stay calm – Sometimes just giving yourself a reminder to stay calm can be helpful.

I will remind myself to stay calm.

5 Take a break – If you are still having trouble staying calm, walk away from the situation for a short time. If another person is waiting for a response from you, tell him/her, "I need a break."

I will take a short break from the situation if I am too angry to share my feelings calmly.

6 Share your feelings – It is important to express your feelings and not keep them bottled up.

I will tell someone that I am angry and why I am angry.

7 Try to find a solution to the situation – After you have shared your feelings with someone else, try to figure out how to fix the situation that made you angry.

I will ask myself questions like: what happened to make me angry, why did it make me angry, how can I make things better, what should I do now.

#BK-371 Simply Social 7™ at School • ©2011 Super Duper® Publications • www.superduperinc.com • 1-800-277-8737

189

Dealing with Anger

Look and Learn

Teacher says: The students in this scene are angry about something that happened at school.

Directions: 1. **Draw a circle** around each student who **is dealing with anger** appropriately.

2. **Draw an X** on each student who **is not dealing with anger** appropriately.

Simply Social 7 **Dealing with Anger**

Think and Review

Directions: Read the stories, and then answer the questions below about the **Simply Social 7** for **Dealing with Anger.**

1. **In the classroom...** Logan's teacher returned the tests that the class took the day before. Logan got an *F* on his test. He was angry, so he tore up his paper.

   Did Logan do the right thing?   a) Yes – What could he do next?

   b) No – What should he have done?

2. **At school...** Amelia tried out for a part in the school musical. When the teacher posted the casting list Amelia saw that she didn't get the part. She was angry, so she took a deep breath, counted to ten, and decided that she would take an acting class and try out again next year.

   Did Amelia do the right thing?   a) Yes – What could she do next?

   b) No – What should she have done?

3. **At home...** Matthew's mom promised to take him to the mall to buy a new baseball glove. Later his mom said they couldn't go because his brother was sick. Matthew was angry, but decided to help his mom make soup for his brother.

   Did Matthew do the right thing?   a) Yes – What could he do next?

   b) No – What should he have done?

4. **In the community...** Sarah wanted to go shopping downtown, but the streets were blocked off for a parade. Sarah was angry, so she knocked over one of the barricades.

   Did Sarah do the right thing?   a) Yes – What could she do next?

   b) No – What should she have done?

Discussion Questions

1. What are some situations in which you had to deal with anger?

2. What would happen if everyone blew up every time they got angry?

Simply Social 7: Dealing with Anger

Take-Home Practice

Dear Parent/Helper,

Today we talked about seven steps to follow when dealing with anger called the **Simply Social 7**. Please review these with your child. Have him/her read or repeat the statement in italics that follows each step. Then sign, date, and return this page. We will add this page to your child's *Simply Social Skills Book!*

Here are the **Simply Social 7** for **Dealing with Anger**...

1. **Recognize that you are angry** – *I will learn to recognize when I am angry so that I will be able to respond appropriately.*

2. **Take a deep breath** – *I will take a deep breath in and let the air out slowly.*

3. **Count to ten** – *I will count to ten and think about how I can calmly talk about the situation.*

4. **Tell yourself to stay calm** – *I will remind myself to stay calm.*

5. **Take a break** – *I will take a short break from the situation if I am too angry to share my feelings calmly.*

6. **Share your feelings** – *I will tell someone that I am angry and why I am angry.*

7. **Try to find a solution to the situation** – *I will ask myself questions like: what happened to make me angry, why did it make me angry, how can I make things better, what should I do now.*

_____   _____   _____
Parent/Helper Signature   Student Signature   Date

- -

Congratulations!

You are a Simply Social Superstar!

Student Directions: After you return the top of this page to your teacher, cut out the award to the right. Add it to the award page in your *Simply Social Skills Book* or to your award wall in your classroom or at home.

Simply Social 7

Using Humor

Simply Social 7 Steps

Teacher says: *Humor* is the ability to understand or express something that is funny. You may have heard the statement, "Laughter is the best medicine." Laughter may not cure a cold or reduce a fever, but it can make you feel better if you are sad or stressed out. Using humor can make unpleasant situations more bearable.

Directions: Teacher will read the **Simply Social 7** steps. Student(s) will read or repeat the statements in italics that follow.

1 **Choose an appropriate time** – Using humor at recess or during lunch is fine, but there are times when humor is not appropriate. For example, you should not be cracking jokes while your teacher is talking.

I will only use humor when it is appropriate.

2 **Look for the humor in an unpleasant situation** – Finding something humorous in an unpleasant situation can improve your mood and help you make it through a difficult time.

I will look for something humorous about an unpleasant situation.

3 **Don't use humor that is hurtful to someone else** – Nobody likes being made fun of or laughed at. When using humor, make sure it is not aimed at someone else.

I will not laugh at or make fun of other people.

4 **Use an expressive voice** – Allow your voice to go higher/lower, louder/softer, and faster/slower as you speak to emphasize the humor in what you are saying.

I will vary the tone, volume, and rhythm of my voice when I am using humor.

5 **Use appropriate body language and facial expressions** – Don't use stiff body language or keep a straight face when you are using humor.

I will make sure my body is relaxed and my facial expressions communicate the humor of my words.

6 **Don't take yourself too seriously** – It's okay to laugh at yourself when you do silly things.

I will not be hard on myself when I do silly things. Instead I will try to laugh at the silly things I do.

7 **Have fun** – Remember that using humor is about having fun. If you're having fun, there's a good chance that the people around you are having fun as well.

I will remember to relax and have fun with my humor.

#BK-371 Simply Social 7™ at School • ©2011 Super Duper® Publications • www.superduperinc.com • 1-800-277-8737   193

Using Humor

Look and Learn

Teacher says: The students in this scene are using humor during the play.

Directions: 1. **Draw a circle** around each student who **is using humor** appropriately.

2. **Draw an X** on each student who **is not using humor** appropriately.

Simply Social 7™

Using Humor

Think and Review

Directions: Read the stories, and then answer the questions below about the **Simply Social 7** for **Using Humor**.

1. **In the classroom...** Evan's classmate, Bobby, has a hard time keeping his desk neat and clean. When Bobby walked by Evan called him "Bob the slob" and everyone laughed.

   Did Evan do the right thing?   a) Yes – What could he do next?

                                              b) No – What should he have done?

2. **At school...** It was raining hard during the school's football game. Rose joked with her friends about how the game looked more like a swim competition than a football game because of all of the water.

   Did Rose do the right thing?   a) Yes – What could she do next?

                                              b) No – What should she have done?

3. **At home...** Aliyah's younger sister doesn't always pronounce her words correctly. When she asked if they were having "bisghetti" for dinner Aliyah laughed at the way her sister said "spaghetti" and made her cry.

   Did Aliyah do the right thing?   a) Yes – What could she do next?

                                              b) No – What should she have done?

4. **In the community...** Ted was visiting a friend in the hospital. He could tell his friend was nervous about having his tonsils taken out, so Ted told his friend a joke he heard at school to take his mind off of the surgery.

   Did Ted do the right thing?   a) Yes – What could he do next?

                                              b) No – What should he have done?

Discussion Questions

1. What are some situations in which you used humor?

2. What would happen if you laughed at people when they made mistakes or had accidents?

Simply Social 7 — Using Humor

Take-Home Practice

Dear Parent/Helper,

Today we talked about seven steps to follow when using humor called the **Simply Social 7**. Please review these with your child. Have him/her read or repeat the statement in italics that follows each step. Then sign, date, and return this page. We will add this page to your child's *Simply Social Skills Book!*

Here are the **Simply Social 7** for **Using Humor**…

1 **Choose an appropriate time** – *I will only use humor when it is appropriate.*

2 **Look for the humor in an unpleasant situation** – *I will look for something humorous about an unpleasant situation.*

3 **Don't use humor that is hurtful to someone else** – *I will not laugh at or make fun of other people.*

4 **Use an expressive voice** – *I will vary the tone, volume, and rhythm of my voice when I am using humor.*

5 **Use appropriate body language and facial expressions** – *I will make sure my body is relaxed and my facial expressions communicate the humor of my words.*

6 **Don't take yourself too seriously** – *I will not be hard on myself when I do silly things. Instead, I will try to laugh at the silly things I do.*

7 **Have fun** – *I will remember to relax and have fun with my humor.*

_____   _____   _____
Parent/Helper Signature   Student Signature   Date

- -

Congratulations!

You are a Simply Social Superstar!

Student Directions: After you return the top of this page to your teacher, cut out the award to the right. Add it to the award page in your *Simply Social Skills Book* or to your award wall in your classroom or at home.

196   #BK-371 Simply Social 7™ at School • ©2011 Super Duper® Publications • www.superduperinc.com • 1-800-277-8737

Simply Social 7 — Dealing with Change

Simply Social 7 Steps

Teacher says: Change is when something is different from the way it used to be. Change can be frightening. It can be scary to do something you've never done before because you don't know what to expect. Change happens all the time, so it's important to learn how to deal with it.

Directions: Teacher will read the **Simply Social 7** steps. Student(s) will read or repeat the statements in italics that follow.

1 **Accept that change is a part of life** – Change happens all of the time. It's part of growing up.

I will remind myself that change is okay and that everyone goes through change many times in life.

2 **Know that change helps us learn and grow** – When something is different you have to adjust to the change. This helps you learn and grow as a person.

I will remember that adjusting to change helps me grow.

3 **Expect change to happen** – If you expect that change is going to happen, it won't catch you off guard when it does.

I will expect that change is going to happen.

4 **See the big picture** – Taking a look at the whole situation can help you understand why the change is necessary.

I will take a step back and look at the whole situation to help me understand the reason for the change.

5 **Don't resist change** – Trying to keep change from happening will cause more stress and anxiety.

I will not cause myself more stress by trying to stop change from happening.

6 **Stay positive** – Try to stay positive when change occurs. Staying positive can reduce the stress caused by the change.

I will decide to remain positive when I am faced with change and look for the good things to come.

7 **Look for new opportunities** – Change gives you a chance to try things you may have never tried before.

I will look for the chance to try new and exciting things.

#BK-371 Simply Social 7™ at School • ©2011 Super Duper® Publications • www.superduperinc.com • 1-800-277-8737

Dealing with Change

Look and Learn

Teacher says: The students in this scene are starting their first day of kindergarten.

Directions: 1. **Draw a circle** around each student who **is dealing with change** appropriately.

2. **Draw an X** on each student who **is not dealing with change** appropriately.

Simply Social 7

Dealing with Change

Think and Review

Directions: Read the stories, and then answer the questions below about the **Simply Social 7** for **Dealing with Change**.

1. **In the classroom...** Christian's teacher was sick and the class had a substitute. Because the substitute did things differently than what he was used to, Christian decided to avoid participating in any activities.

   Did Christian do the right thing?

   a) Yes – What could he do next?

   b) No – What should he have done?

2. **At school...** Shanice was starting her first day at a new school. Because she didn't know her way around the new school building, she decided to make a game out of finding each room that she was looking for.

   Did Shanice do the right thing?

   a) Yes – What could she do next?

   b) No – What should she have done?

3. **At home...** Emily's family moved to a new house. Emily's bedroom in the new house was different from her bedroom in the old house. Emily didn't like it, so she refused to sleep in her new room.

   Did Emily do the right thing?

   a) Yes – What could she do next?

   b) No – What should she have done?

4. **In the community...** When Nathan went to the eye doctor, he found out that his eyes had changed and he needed glasses. Nathan didn't want to wear glasses, so he broke them on purpose and told his mom it was an accident.

   Did Nathan do the right thing?

   a) Yes – What could he do next?

   b) No – What should he have done?

Discussion Questions

1. What are some situations in which you had to deal with change?

2. What would happen if nothing ever changed?

#BK-371 Simply Social 7™ at School • ©2011 Super Duper® Publications • www.superduperinc.com • 1-800-277-8737

199

Simply Social 7: Dealing with Change

Take-Home Practice

Dear Parent/Helper,

Today we talked about seven steps to follow when dealing with change called the **Simply Social 7**. Please review these with your child. Have him/her read or repeat the statement in italics that follows each step. Then sign, date, and return this page. We will add this page to your child's *Simply Social Skills Book!*

Here are the **Simply Social 7** for **Dealing with Change**...

1. **Accept that change is a part of life** – *I will remind myself that change is okay and that everyone goes through change many times in life.*

2. **Know that change helps us learn and grow** – *I will remember that adjusting to change helps me grow.*

3. **Expect change to happen** – *I will expect that change is going to happen.*

4. **See the big picture** – *I will take a step back and look at the whole situation to help me understand the reason for the change.*

5. **Don't resist change** – *I will not cause myself more stress by trying to stop change from happening.*

6. **Stay positive** – *I will decide to remain positive when I am faced with change and look for the good things to come.*

7. **Look for new opportunities** – *I will look for the chance to try new and exciting things.*

_____   _____   _____
Parent/Helper Signature   Student Signature   Date

- -

Congratulations!

You are a Simply Social Superstar!

Student Directions: After you return the top of this page to your teacher, cut out the award to the right. Add it to the award page in your *Simply Social Skills Book* or to your award wall in your classroom or at home.

Notes

Notes